SAVE THREE LIVES

Save Three Lives

A Plan for
Famine Prevention

Robert Rodale
with Mike McGrath

Sierra Club Books   *San Francisco*

Library of Congress Cataloging in Publication Data

Rodale, Robert.
    Save three lives : a plan for famine prevention / by Robert Rodale.
      p.   cm.
    Includes bibliographical references and index.
    ISBN 0-87156-621-4
     1. Alternative agriculture—Developing countries.
    2. Food supply—Developing countries.   3. Organic farming—Developing countries.   4. Agriculture.   I. Title.
    II. Title: Famine prevention.
    S494.5.A65R63   1991
    338.1'62—dc20   91-15224
                                                          CIP

Production by Susan Ristow
Jacket design by Paul Bacon
Book design by David Bullen
Printed on acid-free paper containing a minimum of 50% recovered waste paper, of which at least 10% is post-consumer waste.
10 9 8 7 6 5 4 3 2 1

To our children

That they might know

A world without famine

B. R. & M. M.

Contents

Acknowledgments

It is thanks to John Haberern that you are holding this book in your hands. Head of the nonprofit Rodale Institute, a vice president of Rodale Press and a close friend and associate of Bob Rodale for over thirty years, it was John who had the idea that Bob and I should work on this book together. Both Bob and I thanked him many times for making that connection. And now, we do so once again.

Both Bob and I wanted the book to be as technically accurate as possible; especially those portions that referred to and quoted the work of others. Melissa Meyers, a researcher at Rodale Press, performed an excellent (and extraordinarily time-consuming!) job in this regard.

Carole Piszczek, Julia Hummer, and Mary Lou Schmidt all performed enormous amounts of work, favors, intervention, and coordination that kept this project not only moving but on schedule. Without them, this book would be about half-finished right now.

The staff of our corporate library, unsung heroes of all our endeavors at Rodale Press, once again displayed their ability to not only find anything we wanted but to also introduce us to a few absolutely perfect items we had not even known existed (but once aware of, were unable to live without). Thanks to all who work there.

Thanks also to our editor at the Sierra Club, Jim Cohee, for his encouragement and support. Thanks especially for the letter he sent Bob and me soon after he received the manuscript, a letter that I know made Bob very happy. I'm not exaggerating when I say that one simple letter made all the work we had put into the book worthwhile.

And, of course, thanks to both our families for their tolerance of our absences (and our preoccupation when we *were* around). I know that I have a lot of late nights, early mornings, and Saturdays to pay back (but a more pleasant debt I can't imagine . . .).

And finally, thanks to all those who went before; who have researched natural solutions to agricultural problems; who have documented the problems inherent in "development" and relief; who are out there fighting the good fight; who have devoted their lives to easing the pain of others on a worldwide scale. I only hope that this small effort on our part can make their task a bit easier.

Mike McGrath

In Memoriam:

Robert David Rodale
1930–1990

Back in the spring of 1989, I was asked if I would like to write a book with Bob Rodale. A book about Bob's plan to end world famine, a plan that would encourage people in developing nations to return to the natural forms of farming that were so much more appropriate to their climates and soil conditions than trying to grow chemically fed corn in a desert.

I agreed and began to interview Bob at length about his extensive travels and observations in Third World countries. I thought he was wrong about a couple of major points, but figured I could straighten him out as I helped organize and research the book.

I soon found that many experts were in agreement with Bob's ideas—especially the ideas I was so sure were wrong.

But these experts were speaking in impenetrable language to a tiny audience. Their messages were trapped inside technical journals on library shelves. Bob's goal was to produce the first truly readable book that advocated realistic long-term solutions to hunger and famine.

My research soon convinced me that Bob had the goods. Not

only would his solutions work to ease hunger, they were probably the only solutions that would work.

We finished the first draft, had it fact-checked, fine-tuned the writing, and sent it all off to our editor at the Sierra Club in August of 1990.

"My congratulations," wrote our editor in response. "Your book is the triumph of common sense, and the voice is perfect." Bob and I had both been holding our breath in anticipation of the Sierra Club's response, and our relief was complete. We were, in fact, elated.

You see, we were both used to writing for our own publishing enterprise, Rodale Press; but this was something very different— and deliberately so. One of the first things that Bob had made clear to me is that he wanted this book to be handled by an outside publisher. He didn't want people to see "Rodale Press" on the spine and think that it was a vanity book.

He also wanted that extra shot of endorsement, of acceptance, that would come from having the manuscript pass muster outside of his own company. It was an acceptance—a validation of his ability beyond the company that he had built—that meant very much to him.

Our editor at the Sierra Club wanted a bit more material for the closing chapter, so Bob came up with five pages of great ideas. I dropped those ideas into the conclusion of that chapter (virtually unedited) along with some things we had originally taken out to shorten the text, thinking that we had written too much for that section.

On September 12, 1990, we had a meeting to discuss those additions (we had mailed them off a week or two earlier) and to finalize the business details and format for a second book we had agreed to do together.

Later that day Bob left for Russia.

It was just the latest in a series of trips that Bob had been making to that nation, but this was the one that was to culminate in the achievement of one of his many dreams.

Over the past few years, as the long-term results of heavy chemical use in farming became clearer, representatives of nation after nation had come to the sleepy little town of Emmaus (pronounced E-May-Us) to ask Bob to use his vast storehouse of knowledge of organic agricultural techniques to help them reverse the damage they had done to their land through years of chemical farming.

Bob always said 'yes, of course I'll try and help'. And Russia was to be one of the first to directly benefit from the knowledge that Bob always said he was saving for these nations (who had pretty much created organic agriculture) to rediscover.

He spoke of the Soviets and their devastated farmland often while we worked on this book (which almost included a chapter on the Soviet Union, until we realized that we needed a separate book to tell that story!). "They really need me there," he would say with a very happy smile—and with much honest affection for the Soviet people.

The joint Soviet-Rodale venture that emerged to help that nation's farmers restore their devastated agricultural system with organic growing techniques was just the latest in a series of big ideas that Bob was bringing to reality around the globe.

China was next on the list; their representatives were anxious to get Bob over there working on a similar project. Eastern Europe had its bid in. So did many other nations. In fact, one of the reasons we did this book at this time was to insure that the Third World wasn't overlooked while more developed areas of the globe were jockeying for a better place in line. The world was turning to organic techniques as a solution to the food crisis and they all wanted Bob to be their architect.

The plan that Bob and the Soviets came up with was to publish a Russian language version of the Rodale Institute's award-winning *New Farm* magazine—to provide Soviet farmers with the information they would need to begin their historic transition from chemicals to compost. It was a massive project; one that required Bob and several Rodale chief executives to travel to the Soviet Union many times.

This was pretty much the final trip—the one that would insure that everything was ready for the first issue to make its appearance. The hard work was done.

The negotiations were finished, the necessary (and seemingly endless) permits had all been obtained on previous visits, the stories were in the process of being translated into Russian, and the actual printing was arranged. By all accounts, Bob had the time of his life at the congratulatory banquet in his honor—celebrating with the Russian friends he had grown to view with exceptional affection.

The morning after that banquet—on September 20, 1990—on his way to the airport to begin the long journey home, the van in which Bob Rodale was riding was hit head-on by a bus that swerved to avoid a military vehicle that had suddenly pulled into traffic.

Bob, his translator and the man who was to be the editor of the Russian language version of *New Farm* were all killed instantly.

When I heard the awful news—a buzz of mumbled words, shrieks and people crying—I wandered in a daze until I found myself in Bob's office. I hugged people who were crying, cried with them, and then lit a fire in the woodstove that had sat in the corner of his office for many, many years. A woodstove in the office of the chairman of a quarter-billion dollar company—that was so uniquely Bob.

People came by and saw the fire and were warmed by its sight and I suddenly couldn't bear the thought that it would ever go out.

We found the closet where Bob kept his wood and piled way too many of the small logs into the tiny little stove. It got so hot that Bob's secretaries started taking his papers out of nearby file cabinets out of fear they would catch fire.

Still, we piled on more logs, determined that the fire should never go out.

The next day, the fire was still burning. It had gotten so hot at one point that the protective slate slab underneath the stove had cracked.

A week later, as I was paying my final respects to Bob, the director of the funeral home gestured for me to follow him into a side room.

"You might like to see how they sent him home," he said.

The top of the casket had been covered with a bright blue material that was adorned with swirls of ragged white ribbon held in place by crude, bent staples.

A tribute in tatters. The edges were rough, and yet, there was a beautiful simplicity about this decoration that expressed so much more than if it had been done to American standards of perfection.

It said more eloquently than words ever could what the Russians must have been feeling: "God, we're *so* sorry."

"I don't know where they got the fabric," said a Rodale vice-president who had accompanied Bob on many of his trips to Russia.

The country was just so poor and resources so scarce, he explained, that someone had probably given up their blanket for the blue covering; a valued dress or special-occasion sheet had likely been torn into strips for the ribbon. The heavy industrial staples looked like they had just been removed from a building.

Folk art. A tribute. Found materials. Impossibly achieved delicacy. Love.

Bob had a spirit that inspired people to such actions. And, as I had learned working closely with him over the past year and a half, an intellect and ability that his easy-going manner often shrouded.

Internationally known expert in health and agriculture. Champion skeet shooter who competed in the Olympics and won a gold medal in the Pan-American games in 1967. Loving husband, nurturing father and the perfect fun-filled grandfather.

A man who made a family business grow and thrive by building on the ethics and ideals that had created that company. Who spent millions protecting and developing amaranth—an ancient grain once on the verge of extinction that now has great potential to ease the world's hunger problem.

An avid bicyclist who also built one of the nation's finest facilities for competitive cyclists—the Lehigh County Velodrome. A physical fitness enthusiast who looked much younger than his years.

Protector of the world's environment. Champion of organic agriculture. Vegetarian. Humorist. Community activist. Strategist, planner and manager. Good soul.

And now he's gone.

What can I say? What would *Bob* suggest at this time? How would *he* want us to remember him?

With Bob, you could always expect the unexpected when you asked such a question. (Several of his answers to seemingly simple questions gave me whiplash!)

But my guess is that Bob would urge us to try and learn something from his passing.

And what I learned—and learned hard—is that you can never really be *sure* that you'll ever see someone again. So it's best not to leave business undone; feelings unspoken.

Bob's passing has taught me that we when we say goodbye to someone, it may well be the last time we see that person. It *probably* won't be; but it *could* be.

Anyone who walks out a door just might be walking out of your life. Forever.

So pay a compliment. Don't save something nice you've been meaning to say to someone. Tell them that you think they're a good, talented person; that you value their friendship; that you admire their ability; that they make you happy.

It's an action that you'll never regret.

And you'll have picked up one final bit of wisdom from a man who spent his life trying to enrich the lives of others.

Mike McGrath
Emmaus, Spring 1991

Part One

The Problem: *Why* Famine Is a Threat to Us All

CHAPTER ONE

The People

They're not at all like you'd expect. And that's because the television images you've seen just don't tell their whole story. The people of Africa are *not* like you see on TV. Those images—bloated bellies, the starving children under attack by an army of flies—don't capture what these people are really about.

I was talking to a friend about this book recently and mentioned that I wanted to devote the first chapter to helping the reader understand the people whom famine threatens. I said that I felt a tremendous responsibility to get across what these people are truly like; to try to explain the essence of their day-to-day existence. He had *just* gotten up and wasn't really awake yet, so his response wasn't thought out or calculated. What he said was more like one of those word association tests where you say the first thing that enters your mind.

"Rickets and flies," were his words.

He didn't mean anything negative by it. In fact, by the sorrow in his voice, I could tell that he thought I had set myself an impossible task. The pictures of Third World famine victims that had invaded his living room had crushed a part of his spirit. To him, these were people who were beyond help. If you thought about them long enough, you'd start to cry. Their plight, their hopelessness, their sheer, crushing numbers, were all just too much for him. And, I suspect, for many of you as well.

But I don't feel that way. I don't think that reversing—and eventually preventing—this trend toward famine is impossible. And I *know* that these images do not convey an accurate idea of what these people are like. It's certainly not what I see in my own mind when I think about the people who are at risk of falling prey to famine. But then, I have an advantage over the average American. I've *been* to Africa. I've walked in the Sahel and other famine-prone areas. I've also visited with struggling farmers in Costa Rica, Asia, and the USSR, and I've been a guest in some of the poorest homes in Mexico.

Having spent time with these people and having traveled throughout much of what we call the "Third World," I am always surprised by the sameness of the photos and film images that find their way into American homes. Yes, these heart-wrenching, spirit-crushing pictures are accurate portrayals of what graceful, talented and loving people probably look like in their final hour. But those images are no more accurate a record of what these people *truly* are than a deathbed photo would be of my life or of yours.

What's the worst you've ever looked? Imagine a photo of you taken a few minutes after you regained consciousness following major surgery. A videotape of you being pulled, bleeding, from a wrecked car. Or, if you've ever suffered from a drug or alcohol problem, a visual record of you at your lowest point.

Would that really be you? The *real* you? The person inside who represents you at your best—the parent, the spouse, the singer, the writer, the painter, the sports fan, the friend? I don't think so. The image *is* a small part of you, of course. But you in jeopardy—in pain, in fear, at risk. That image may only represent the tiniest fraction of the smallest portion of your life—but once captured on film and shown to others, it will be what they think of you, how they remember you. In their minds that image will become "you." But it's not. You're much more than that. And so are the people this book is about.

The reason this book is being written—the reason I am devoting so much of my life, time, and resources to the goal of famine prevention—is the people in those horrible, gut-wrenching pictures we see. But not them at that frozen moment in time. Not them captured at their worst imaginable instant, their lowest point. Not them as they linger at the gates of death. Because, sadly, something that most of us—especially those with any kind of medical background—realize is that it is too late for the people in those pictures. The time for driver education is not after the crash. A bullet-proof vest isn't much help after you've been shot. The people in those pictures—with the faces and the bellies and, yes, the "rickets and flies"—that move us to pick up the phone, call an 800 number, and read our credit card information to someone at the other end, are often already dead. They're usually beyond our help.

But imagine, if you will, being able to stop the cars *before* they crash, to put on the vest before the bullet hits, to prevent the hunger before it begins. You do have that power. You have the ability to *really* save people who, I assure you, are proud, happy, vibrant—joyous is actually the best word to describe them. Yes, joyous. These people, on a normal day-to-day basis, are happier than you or I, happier than the average American or European. And that little-known happiness, that "other side" of these people who are unseen in America until they are in their final hour, is why I'm talking to you now. I have a powerful need to share with you the *reality* of these people. But, in doing so, I realize that I'm going squarely against the grain of conventional wisdom.

Starving babies get results. Nobody ever went broke showing the kinds of images we're talking about. Whether you're a religious broadcaster seeking contributions or an international aid organization in the midst of a fund-raising drive, you get the best results when you show the bleakest pictures. Bring on the starving children, the 60-pound adults, and in the same motion, people turn away from the TV screen or the printed page and reach for their wallets. The technique works. The ploy is effective. But it's wrong. Not wrong in the sense that such appeals exploit the people themselves (although consider how you'd feel if those images of you at your worst that we discussed earlier were beamed into millions of homes in order to "help" you), but wrong because it's too late to really achieve anything once hunger has gone that far.

I believe those appeals are wrong because they aren't showing you those same people at an earlier, less critical point, when your help could really have made a difference. The pitch I would make would show you poor but happy people sitting around an indoor campfire sharing food with a stranger. My pitch would show you villagers dancing on a feast day, and healthy mothers hugging smiling children. And I would end by asking you to help keep these people from becoming "those" people—the ones in the pictures we just can't stand to look at for long. Admittedly, my approach is a hard sell. But if you truly want your money or your work or your food, or whatever it is you choose to give, to do any good, it's the only true sell. Because the only way you can really help these people is to literally go back in time and *prevent* the famine—prevent the problems that forced them to abandon their lands and their lives to make an ill-advised death march toward refugee camps where there is often no food but there always seem to be plenty of cameras.

Sometimes I think that people just don't understand how hunger and malnutrition really work. Some Americans seem to associate the whole process with the popular movie plot where the hero is poisoned and told he has twenty-four hours to find the antidote before the poison finishes him off. We've all seen that story a dozen times. We know he's still going to be running around energetically looking for the antidote at least twenty-three and a half hours later. As long as he finds it in the final twenty-nine minutes (which he's sure to do), he'll be O.K.

But poisons don't work like that, of course, outside of Hollywood. In real life, our hero would be in pretty bad shape after about six hours, probably unable to move after twelve, and 99 percent dead by the time his Hollywood counterpart is just starting to get down to business. Starvation, unfortunately, follows the real life, not the movie, model. You can't come charging in at the last minute, knock the bad guy to the ground, gulp down the antidote, and make everything all right.

With the devastating conditions caused by famine-induced hunger, even if you do get the right food to the refugee camps in amounts large enough to do any good, even if you do provide enough clean water for drinking and for preparing that food, and even if there is equipment to distribute that food, all you succeed in doing is freezing the picture. You can't reverse it like a videotape. People who have gone too long without food and water suffer permanent damage. Blindness is a common result of coming back from the brink. So is lameness: Few things are more tragic than legs that will never again be strong enough to support their owner.

And then, of course, you have to face the problem of what to do with the people you save. Should you send them back to the barren lands they fled so they can turn around and return again, like some sort of ghostly commuters? Can you build housing and hospitals for them and provide an endless stream of food and supplies?

Of course not. But I must be careful about how this is phrased. To be perceived as being against emergency famine relief could breed instant comparisons with Adolf Hitler. So let me assure you that I am not against emergency relief. No human being can be. To react to those harrowing images with immediate donations reinforces our humanity. There would be something wrong with us if we didn't care, if we didn't flinch yet try to help at the same time.

The message I need to get across is that *we can do more.* We can, in a sense, climb into that time machine. We can go back before the march to the camp where death waits, before the harvest failed. My only fear is that without the frightful images, without the swollen bellies of once-beautiful babies, we will falter. I'm afraid that, without those images to shock us into action, we won't see the importance of what needs to be done. That is my biggest fear. Sometimes it's as paralyzing as the images themselves.

I need your help. You've already begun to give it by listening to me so far, and I apologize if I've taken too long to set the stage. Perhaps that's a reaction to my fear that I won't explain this well enough—that I'll let these wonderful people down. That I won't be able to keep them off that dusty road to the death camps. So please help me. If I falter, pick me up and let's keep going. If you spot an error in something I say, tell me. If I make a suggestion or endorse someone else's ideas and you see a way that those concepts can be improved, please tell me.

And now, much further along than I intended, let me take you to a couple of places. Let's meet some people. Real people, not pictures.

My first contact with people in a developing country was in 1949. I was nineteen years old, and my father was pressing me to come to work. He had asked me to take a light load that semester in college so that I could spend more time in the family business. I said yes, as long as I could take a trip somewhere first. He gave me a couple hundred dollars, and I spent six weeks driving around Mexico by myself.

I loved it. Other people might have felt uncomfortable being in what were some pretty primitive places. But listening to my father and his friends talk had led me to believe that, when it comes to a healthy environment, primitive is often better than modern—especially when it comes to food. Someone from the United States might look at Mexicans and say, "They are just eating corn, beans, and all these odd plants that are growing wild. That's not nearly as good as the hamburgers and french fries we get to eat." But my outlook even back then was to recognize that they were eating much more nutritious food than the average North American. Plus, I personally like that kind of food. I do now and I did then.

The primitive food of Mexico is really natural food. Not natural in the sense of a word on a box that may or may not mean anything, but really natural—whole food, grown close to the people who eat it, and in tune with their nature. Natural foods (which, by the way, happen to be the cornerstone of our famine prevention plan) from plants that thrive naturally in the area. They don't have to be bred, imported, or genetically altered to provide nutritious food. In some cases, those plants aren't even deliberately planted. They're just there. They grow wild, and centuries of trial and error have revealed their uses to the people they surround.

But I'm getting ahead of myself. I promised to introduce you to the people—the people who made me want to prevent famines in the first place. My mother had a new car, and (foolishly, now that I think about it) she let me borrow it. I had a friend who was going to come with me, but he bailed out at the last minute and I said, "All right, I'll go by myself!" It just didn't occur to me to be worried or afraid, and because I wasn't afraid, there was no reason to be.

In 1949, you couldn't drive to Mexico and *not* be exposed to life in primitive cultures. There were no superhighways. I was basically traveling through one Third World region after another. And, of course, just to keep things interesting, I couldn't speak any Spanish! How's that for being an "innocent abroad"?

But it didn't matter. There were always at least a few people around who spoke a little English. They'd see me, the obvious young American boy, and immediately remember that they knew someone who needed a ride to the next town. And so I'd oblige them and ended up being a welcome guest in simple home after simple home.

After a while, I was able to make out a few words—mostly greetings, goodbyes, and the names of some foods. But even without understanding the language, I knew I was experiencing a very good feeling. It's hard *not* to have a good feeling when people who are smiling all the time are feeding you. The rides I gave didn't begin to repay the food, entertainment, and hospitality I enjoyed in these simple homes. I've always felt I owed these people something for the good care they took of me, the joy they shared with me. I wonder how many visitors to our country would feel the same?

In 1968 I was back in Mexico for the Olympics, and I got in the habit of walking down a certain street near the Olympic Village to a bakery. Back then, a Mexican bakery was a wonderful place. You entered this big room where you were surrounded by shelves loaded with hundreds of different kinds of pastries and other things. You got a tray and tongs and walked around until your tray was filled; then you packed it all up and paid for it.

In 1968, at least in this village, all the bakery goods were the same kind as I remembered from my trip when I was nineteen. The pastries were wonderful—very delicious despite being very low in sugar. My favorite was a big cookie that was just a little sweeter than bread. I bought a whole bunch, took them back to the guys at the Olympic Village, and asked them what they thought. They said, "This is no good. It isn't sweet!"

Ten years later I again went back to Mexico, and now everything in the bakery was loaded with sugar. Between 1949 and 1968, very little had changed. People were still eating delicious, healthy "natural" food. But between 1968 and 1978, it seemed like the diet of the whole nation had changed. They had lost that sense of natural goodness in their foods. They were eating almost as badly as we do in the United States.

I realize I've strayed off a bit here, but the truth is that I can't get that Mexican bakery out of my head. In a strange sort of way, it's become a symbol of what's happened throughout the parts of the globe that we call the "Third World" or the "developing countries." The reasons behind that bakery's demise are the same reasons why we now find it necessary to prevent famines. For I honestly believe that much of the misery, the hunger, and the terrible environmental problems that these people are facing is due to the "sugarization" of their cultures. Much of the famine that we see on TV is the direct result of international "aid" that has tried to make them more like us—even when they were perfectly happy just the way they were. (Please don't think I'm just a ranting environmentalist. Later in the book we'll quote hundreds of high-level officials who agree that outside efforts to "develop" impoverished nations have led directly to the crisis we face today. And some of those officials would have choked on their words a decade ago.)

What happened to that wonderful Mexican bakery is what I fear happens all too often when relief agencies go in to "help" native peoples. Instead of improving what's already there—instead of taking something that's good and helping to make it better—this "aid" wipes out everything native to the area and replaces it with things that are more American, more European. Unfortunately, that often simply means adding a lot of sugar.

When I was in Zimbabwe a few years ago, a man I was working with showed me a study—the results of interviews, actually, with small farmers in the region. They had been asked how they felt about the food they were growing and eating and about the advice they got from the extension service.

Now, at that time, Zimbabwe had become fairly advanced for a Third World country. A lot of modern agricultural science had taken hold. Groups of experts had come in and said, "Here's high-quality corn and a better variety of wheat. Plant these and don't waste your time on all those odd little plants you've been growing for hundreds of years. It's just not an efficient way to farm." But the survey showed that the people weren't all that happy with their new "prosperity." In fact, they were complaining. They told these experts that they were angry because they had lost their native plants and they rattled off the names of all the specific plants they had lost. The experts were surprised, to say the least. From their point of view, there was more food now. What could be wrong?

Basically, the people were saying, "We don't feel as good as we used to feel. We can't cope with disease as well. In the past, whenever our children would get sick, we would take a part of one of our special plants, prepare it the way we were taught, give it to them, and they would get better. But now we don't have those plants anymore. You made us pull them up so that we could grow more corn.

"When we ourselves got sick, we used to eat this or eat that—but we don't have those plants anymore, either. And now none of us feels as good as we used to feel—even though we have more food."

Did some of those native plants have true medicinal powers? Or was the effect merely psychological—generation after generation passing along stories of which parts of what plants to eat when you weren't feeling well, until expectation alone became enough to make people feel better? I don't know the answer to that question, of course, but more importantly, I don't think that it really matters. What does matter is that these special plants—vitally important as culture and comfort to the people in their area—were completely ignored by the experts who came in to "help." Now, many of the plants are gone—perhaps forever—and the people miss them.

Some of you may be thinking, "Such ignorant savages, missing something they probably didn't need to begin with! And they're not even grateful about all this extra corn and wheat they have now." But that's a pretty shortsighted view. Chances are that at least one or two of those native plants did have a real medical use. But we'll never get to study the plants or learn to use them ourselves because the plants are gone. Actually, the fact that the people miss those "old" plants isn't ignorance at all. I think it reflects a strong instinctive intelligence on their part, telling them that something tremendously important is missing in their lives. And, finally, I believe that such people, though living in a country overflowing with corn and wheat, are more famine prone now than when they were only growing a few such "cash crops" and devoting the rest of their land and energy to the old native plants they'd been relying on for centuries when times were bad.

Corn and wheat are not native to the areas we're talking about. The imported, highly selected strains being grown in the Third World are tremendously artificial. They've been bred, standardized, and altered to the point that they're not what I'd refer to as "natural" plant life. They have tremendously high water and fertilizer needs—especially the corn that covers much of Africa these days. As long as these people have experts supplying them with seed, farm machinery, fuel, fertilizer, and the equipment to dig new wells when the old ones run dry, they're "fine"—at least until they begin to suffer the natural consequences of growing one crop over and over again in the same place too long. By using enough chemical fertilizer, you can pretty much manage to grow corn anywhere, but the soil itself gets worse and worse after every harvest.

Since nothing lasting is ever being added to it, it shrinks. It turns gray instead of the rich black it's supposed to be. It doesn't hold water as well as "real" soil. And what little real soil remains is blown away by the wind or washed off by the heavy seasonal rains.

And, of course, whenever you grow too much of any one thing, you risk a devastating blight. All you need is to have an insect pest become resistant to the insecticides you're constantly spraying—and the more you expose a pest to a particular insecticide, the faster it will build up a resistance. Or a resistant strain of disease can suddenly appear and wipe out your entire crop. Did you know that such a blight wiped out the majority of the corn crop in the United States just not that long ago? In 1970, a "devastating fungus" appeared and spread quickly through America's corn crop, infecting large areas and threatening to destroy the following year's harvest completely. A 1989 report by the National Academy of Sciences provides these details:

> The epidemic . . . caught the nation unprepared. . . . Within six months, this wind-borne disease was blighting fields from Maine to Miami, Moline to Mobile.
>
> In severely diseased areas, clouds of spores boiled blackly over the combine harvesters to infect miles of downwind fields. . . . For an infected field, there was no practical treatment.
>
> The Corn Belt almost came unbuckled. Nearly 20% of the nation's crop was destroyed; most of the rest was threatened. In southern states, more than half was lost.

The corn that fell prey to this billion-dollar blight did so because it was highly standardized; "genetically uniform" are the words used by the NAS. An article in the British journal *New Scientist* (which estimates that the United States lost *half* of its corn crop that year), explains that "most varieties of corn then grown in the U.S. had a single gene that made them susceptible to the disease."

Like the "Green Revolution" supercrops we'll discuss in coming chapters, America's corn was vulnerable because it was so far removed from its ancient, naturally occurring ancestors that had developed natural resistance to such diseases. Luckily, many of those original strains had been saved for research. By going back to species of wild corn that had wisely been preserved, researchers found strains that naturally resisted the blight.

But rather than acknowledge that half a country planted with a single strain of field corn wasn't such a great idea, the people in charge simply treated the symptom and didn't address the problem. As the NAS pointed out in 1972, "the key lesson of 1970 is that genetic uniformity is the basis of vulnerability to epidemics." But nobody chose to learn that lesson. The people in charge of U.S. agricultural policy instead took an "aspirin" so that the immediate headache of this specific blight would go away. They chose not to take steps that would prevent future headaches—steps such as encouraging mixed plantings in place of the dangerous monoculture farming system we use to tempt famine to our shores.

Farmers who "put all their eggs in one basket" by not growing a diversity of foods are taking a huge risk. If you grow twenty different crops on your twenty acres and something kills all your corn, you're still going to get by. If you've got twenty acres of corn alone, you're in serious trouble.

But rather than encouraging people in the Third World to diversify for safety's sake, most of the experts are instead urging them to plant massive amounts of so-called cash crops, such as wheat and corn. In their view, such a system is "safe," because there's a well-established market for such crops. In reality, the price a farmer can get for corn or wheat is often extremely low. And, in such a system, growing costs are always going to be high. But there is a well-established market. The experts can call its number up on their computer screens. They can match their growth projections with the actual figures. So they call it "safe."

But, of course, it's *not* safe. It's an accident waiting to happen. It's a fragile system that also pollutes the land and water with huge amounts of chemicals—many of which aren't even allowed to be used any more in the country (often ours) that manufactures them.

(Of course, that doesn't mean you won't wind up eventually eating corn or wheat that's been grown with those banned chemicals. One of the saddest facts is that food grown in Third World countries with such destructive techniques often doesn't even go to feed local people. It's exported to satisfy massive foreign debts. And it may wind up on *your* table after it's been imported. That's also something we'll discuss in another chapter.)

What really boggles the mind is that the system being forced on many people in famine-prone areas of the world is the same one— grow a lot of corn with a lot of chemicals—that's already not working all that well right here in America's much more fertile soils. Our farms are being foreclosed in record numbers. The chemicals that keep worn-out soil producing are so expensive that farmers can't sell their crops for what it cost to grow them. And, of course, those chemicals have wreaked havoc with our drinking water supplies.

If we can't make such "good old American know-how" work in America, how can we expect it to work in parts of the world where so many more people need to be fed per acre? Where it costs even more to drag all those chemicals and machines to the farms? Where there aren't even any roads to get the fertilizer and chemicals in or the corn out?

So, is my plan to simply stop planting miles of corn and instead encourage Third World people to go back to cultivating native plants? Plants that don't require imported seed, machines, and chemicals to grow; that are much better at surviving droughts and that make the people feel better just by being around?

Such a plan does seem to be almost too simple, doesn't it? But it is that very simplicity and common sense that makes me believe that this *is* the approach to follow.

Certainly, some corn could be planted. In fact, our system would build up the land so that, after a few years, a nice corn crop could be grown every couple of years *without* chemical fertilizers and pesticides. We know—we've done it ourselves in test plots on our own research farm and in places like Africa and Costa Rica.

It is such a simple, and yet such a forward-looking solution that I *know* we can do this. If we change the entire way we deal with these people who are at risk of famine—the way we encourage them to use their land—we can take a huge step toward ending famine today.

But if this message is so simple and so logical, why don't the experts—the policymakers—hear it? Maybe I can help answer that by telling you the story about the "improved stoves." Such stoves have been an essential element of most plans to ease the firewood crisis in Africa. Because people cut down too much wood for their fires, the experts propose that we sell them inexpensive, efficient stoves that use less wood. That's the plan. Makes sense, right?

Not if you've ever actually sat around an African indoor campfire. One thing I quickly noticed on my travels is that the smoke from the fire kills the bugs that would otherwise eat their way through the thatched roof of the hut.

In fact, some families even store food up in the rafters so that it is preserved by the smoke. And, of course, you have to realize that fires are a necessary component of most mealtimes. In a land without refrigeration (indeed, a land mostly without electricity itself in the rural areas we're concerned with), every meal must be cooked fresh. No fire, no food.

And that same fire also serves as entertainment—the people use their fires to relax at night. After coming home from a hard day's work, they make a fire to cook food and to enjoy watching the flames—which are very interesting. *I* certainly enjoy watching them. Before you try to change things, you have to understand that the fire itself is an integral part of their society. It's something that's been imprinted on them, something that's been a part of their basic culture for hundreds of thousands of years. It's their television set. (Actually, since my travels in Africa I've come to look at it more the other way around. I think television is *our* electronic campfire, our way of trying to reclaim that feeling of warmth and simple entertainment. Their campfire isn't really their form of television, it's a *real* campfire—the pure essence of what we're trying to reclaim with television, which is often a poor substitute.)

But the experts decide that fires are bad because the people cut down too many trees to feed the flames. And so their solution to this very real firewood problem is to use what they call "appropriate technology." They offer to sell the people high-efficiency cookstoves.

And, of course, nobody buys the new stoves. Not just because they don't have the money—although they don't, of course. But because, in many of the cultures where these stoves are offered, the fire serves *many* needs. Fire entertains the people, provides light and warmth, enriches their lives, and kills the bugs that would otherwise eat the roof from over their heads—all while it cooks dinner. How's a modern stove going to compare with that?

The people look at the stove, and they don't see improvement. They notice that there are no visible flames, that it doesn't give off enough light, that it doesn't send off enough smoke to kill the bugs in the roof. They say, "This is a poor substitute!" And, for them, it truly is. The stove just does one job. It does the job O.K., and with less wood. But the campfire did four or five jobs—*all* of them well!

We recognize that the firewood problem is severe. In fact, a few chapters from now we'll explain how the overharvesting of firewood has actually hurt food production directly. (And also—in the chapter devoted to women—we'll show how this Third World fuel crisis has contributed to the overpopulation problem that these nations suffer.)

And, because we've been there—because we've seen and felt

what the home fire means—and because we understand these crucial connections between firewood, food, and population, we realize more than anyone that the wood problem must be solved. But
our solution takes the culture into account. Rather than decide to
change a people's centuries-old lifestyle for them (and, by ignorance, take the very roof off their heads), we found a way to feed
those fires without any ecological or social side effects. Our proposal—which is really nothing more than an improved version of
what the people themselves did centuries ago—allows the rich tradition of fire to continue. And no one has to cut down trees to keep
those fires burning.

As you'll see in Chapter 6 (on alley cropping), there's a simple,
natural solution that also provides free natural fertilizer, stakes and
poles, food for people and animals, and the raw material for several
prescription drugs. (Now *there's* a cash crop!)

But I'm getting ahead of myself again. I keep wanting to tell you
more of my experiences with these wonderful people, to take you
with me into their huts. I keep getting distracted by their plight, by
the problems that "solutions" foisted on them by experts have
caused. Let's try again.

I was staying at a professor's house in a part of Africa where almost
everyone speaks Swahili. However, just like when I was a young
man in Mexico, I didn't speak the language. In fact, I knew only one
word in Swahili. It sounded exactly like *Missouri,* like the state of
Missouri. It's a very pleasant, friendly word. Basically it means
"Everything's okay—I'm doing just fine, thanks."

There were farms in the nearby hills, and one afternoon I decided to walk up and take a look at some of them. There was no
road, just a heavily used foot trail. A mountain biker would probably love it. There *were* several people with bikes, but they were
pushing them, not riding!

I walked for quite a way, passing a lot of people who were carrying firewood back down, and then a man who was about forty
years old came toward me, wearing a well-worn T-shirt. He just
buttonholed me, rattling away at me in Swahili. I knew he figured
any white man that far up in the hills must know Swahili. And I'm
ashamed to admit that, while most white people in the area *do*
know the language, I didn't; and it didn't seem to dawn on him that
I couldn't respond or even understand what he was talking about.
So, after this had gone on for a while, I said the only word I knew—
which was *masuri*. He laughed and everything just seemed to come
together. It made him, and me, tremendously happy. Then he
smiled, waved goodbye and walked away.

I can't begin to describe the sensation that left me with. It's hard
to explain how, but for me his attitude expressed the goodness and
niceness that seems to permeate every "primitive" or "developing"
culture I've visited. I wish I could take you up into those hills with
me. I know that no words can ever explain the sheer joy and good
feelings that come from an encounter like that. So many Americans
never have the chance to meet these kinds of people. Even if they
do go to a Third World country, they're so appalled by the poverty
they see in the cities that they never get a chance to see the people
who still live on the land.

They've never said "Missouri" to a native on the side of a mountain and gotten a smile back as big as the sky. They've never been
entertained by a smoldering fire while it cooked their dinner *and*
performed pest control duty all at once.

The intellectuals, the academic people—they look at computer
screens with a maze of figures and symbols on them and they really
don't see the connection to the *people*. Sometimes I've gotten the
impression from some of the experts I've met that they don't even
like the people they're supposedly trying to help. They're just
trying out this system they designed in Iowa or Denmark or Oxford, and they'd just as soon there weren't any people involved at

all. It's sad, but in many cases, native people are merely an annoyance to the development experts. Instead of being seen as the reason that these experts are there (which, of course, is precisely the case; in a way it's the people who are providing work and employment for these experts) the people are all too often viewed as the reason that this miraculous system the experts have devised isn't working the way it did back in the lab.

And even the experts who honestly would like the people—who might even learn from them—are afraid to mingle with them. Not afraid for their lives or anything like that, but afraid of losing their "objectivity." They say, "If I meet these people and they become my friends, it'll bias my judgment." So they insulate themselves from the people. That way, they don't have to face up to the cold reality that the "development" they're pushing either ignores or will destroy much of the culture of these people. And, of course, the even sadder fact that if their plan doesn't succeed, it will leave the people worse off than before—with a foreign system that doesn't work and with no native plants and techniques to fall back on.

So here am I, the voice in the wilderness, calling out, "Hey, look! You don't need all these shiploads of things to help these people to feed themselves. They have all the resources they need right here around them. Why don't you just look?" These people can easily feed themselves. All they need is for outsiders to stop telling them to try to farm a desert as if it were the wheatfields of the U.S. Midwest—and perhaps a little bit of help, mostly in the form of information on how to use their own natural resources a bit more efficiently.

Someday, the ships that bring all the chemicals and equipment that allow large-scale U.S.-style farming in arid lands will almost certainly stop coming. After all, the countries that have to foot the bill for sending all that stuff aren't in such hot shape themselves these days. And the Third World roads that are already falling apart will almost certainly become impassable—that seems to be a matter of universal agreement. Some people, amazingly, still talk about spending untold billions to rebuild them—despite strong evidence that such roads can never be maintained.

But you don't need ships. And you don't need roads. That's the essence of our solution. It avoids massive imports of chemicals and machinery. It realizes that the people in need don't even live near these roads that are unusable. Everything these people need to ensure survival—to prevent famine—is already there, right where they live.

"Bob's Village"

I fear that I'm doing a poor job. I wanted to show what the people we're talking about are really like, and I keep getting off the track. Here's my last chance. It's the story I told my editor, Mike McGrath, when we first discussed this part of the book. Since then, he keeps calling it "Bob's village." Of course, the village is not "mine" in any sense of the word. But it truly is one of my favorite places in the world.

It's in the province of Morales, which is just south of Mexico City. A little village called Otopec. I was there three years ago, and had an experience that I wish everyone could have. Nothing exciting or earthshaking happened. Nothing that would have made the evening news. But Otopec is such a joyful place—such happy people—that after visiting there you could never think about destroying native culture in the name of "progress," or think of people who choose to live close to the earth as "primitive."

The streets are not terribly inviting. In fact, they are barely navigable. They are all torn up and full of potholes. Someone driving from Cuervaco to Tepathon—the major cities on either side of the village—wouldn't think of stopping in Otopec, because it looks like a poor collection of adobe houses. But what looks like a "poor" mud hut is paradise inside. The doorway is realy just an open spot in a wall, leading to a little compound. The first thing you notice is that there are beautiful trees *inside*. The hut is not really a house the way we think of one. Since there are few insect problems, almost everything is open to the air. Some rooms are enclosed, of course, but mostly things are out in the open.

Yes, by our standards the people are poor, but they have 100 feast days a year! They grab more joy and celebration out of life than we could ever imagine.

I was there on a Sunday afternoon—it was a feast day, of course—and we were watching a group of boys—about ten or twelve years old—learn to dance. Dressed in jeans, belts, and hats, they were doing a kind of cowboy dance—a traditional Mexican cowboy dance.

We must have sat there for an hour watching them dance, and I thought to myself, "This is not the way I would spend a Sunday at home." I would probably be working or out riding my bike. The last thing I would do is watch something like this—unless my own son or grandson was involved, of course. But here I was just sitting and watching—and surprised at how relaxed and good it made me feel.

Now, this was not a tourist kind of event. Again, this was not a place where tourists came. There were no chairs. We were all sitting on the curb with the local people. Suddenly it dawned on me that I was witnessing some kind of contest. There was a man who seemed to be in charge, and I now realized that he was the judge— he was going to decide who could dance the best. The boys were not doing the dance all that well, but you could tell that they had been practicing, and that they *wanted* to do it. They weren't forced to participate. A part of their culture was being passed down from one generation to the next, and they were an active part of it. And yet, they really didn't seem to be in competition the way American kids would be. When one of the boys was finally declared the winner, he didn't put his hands up in the air and yell "Great!" or anything.

The prize, by the way, was a pair of spurs. I had figured that out when I noticed that none of the kids was wearing spurs and the man in charge was holding a pair in his hands. I guessed then that he was going to decide who was best and give him those spurs. I realized all this about a half-hour before he actually picked the winner, and for the rest of the contest I sat there mesmerized. I was thoroughly enjoying myself watching them dance, trying to figure out who was the best and how he would react when the winner was announced. I had more interest in that little native contest than in the final game of the World Series.

And then it was over. There was one boy who was obviously a little better than the others, and the man just gave him the spurs without any kind of fanfare. Maybe I imagined it, but the youngster almost looked embarrassed. He took the spurs and didn't say anything. He just had a kind of half-smile on his face. And that was it. Everybody went back to their families. Nobody went away saying "We've got to beat him next year and get those spurs back," or anything like that. It was a wonderfully relaxing, low-key kind of thing.

These cultures are just full of occasions like that. Occasions that are very meaningful to the people and enjoyable for us if viewed through their eyes—their perspective. These are things that we should never try to change, or allow our aid to accidentally destroy.

These cultures and their people are very fragile. They could easily be destroyed by the "success" of a more Western way of life. You'd go back a couple of years later and they'd be watching the Super Bowl on a satellite broadcast instead.

There's a section in Graham Greene's wonderful book *Journey Without Maps* (about his travels in wild, underdeveloped areas) that

I'd like to share with you. He describes the people he met in native villages, and the difference between what he saw and what Europeans had assured (and warned) him that these people would be like:

> Their laughter and their happiness seemed the most courageous things in nature. Love, it has been said, was invented in Europe by the troubadours, but it existed here without the trappings of civilization.
>
> They were tender towards their children (I seldom heard a crying child and never saw one beaten), they were tender towards each other in a gentle, muffled way; they didn't scream or "rag" in shrill speech. . . . One was aware the whole time of a standard of courtesy to which it was one's responsibility to conform.
>
> And these were the people one had been told . . . that one couldn't trust. "A black will always do you down."
>
> It was no good protesting later that one had not come across a single example of dishonesty; . . . only gentleness, kindness, an honesty which one would not have found in Europe.
>
> It astonished me that I was able to travel through an unpoliced country with twenty-five men who knew that my money box contained what to them was a fortune in silver. We were not in British or French territory now; it wouldn't have mattered . . . if we had disappeared. We couldn't even count as armed; the automatic was hidden in the money box, never loaded. . . . It would have been easy when we were crossing one of the fibre bridges to stage an accident.
>
> But I wasn't "done"; there wasn't an instance of even the most petty theft, though in every village the natives swarmed into the hut where all day my things were lying about, soap (to them very precious), razor, brushes.

Greene relates how the European "keepers of the local wisdom" warn that "You can have a boy for ten years and he'll do you at the end of it"—wisely observing that they say this as they themselves prepare to "do" someone "in the proper commercial way" that morning.

Wonderful stuff. But the passage that always gets to me—that expresses the feeling I wanted to get across to you in this chapter—comes a few sentences later. Greene reaches a native village hours later than he had planned. Darkness had already fallen, and he's obviously relieved to have reached *any* destination. He soon realizes, however, that this isn't just any destination. There is a feeling of home, of warmth here: "All the fires had been lit in the huts and the smoke blew across the narrow paths stinging the eye; but the little flames were like home; they were the African equivalent of the lights behind red blinds in English villages."

Exactly. "The little flames were like home." It would not be progress, it would not be development by any definition to snuff out those flames, because you'd snuff out the home as well.

In his excellent critique of relief programs, "The Politics of Food Aid" (1988), famine expert Lloyd Timberlake talks about his travels in hunger-plagued lands. The dilemma he describes is one that I myself have faced, and it is one of the reasons that I am writing this book. I'll let Lloyd explain:

> I gained weight while conducting a survey of the poorest and hungriest families in the slums of Bangladesh, because it would have been a great dishonor to them if they had not offered me food and drink once I crossed their thresholds; and there was, of course, no way such hospitality could be refused.
>
> I had similar experiences in the Ethiopian highlands during the famine in 1984, where guests were fed, though local people died of hunger.

Lloyd uses this as an introduction to the "even less logical" manner in which food transactions between nations occur. With his larger argument, I'm in complete agreement: Relief programs only fuel long-term famine. But in these instances that he uses as example, I think he has missed the point. Yes, his arguments about the problems associated with relief programs make a strong case for such aid actually being a prime cause of famine. And yet he has failed to see the faces of the people he works so hard to help.

Is pride in home and village foolish? Is clinging to your way of life, your tradition, despite hunger and poverty, something to be changed? No, Lloyd. The seemingly foolhardy generosity of these wonderful people, their stubborn pride in clinging to their way of life, is why I am here now. Yes, these people must be fed. They must be helped to recover the methods by which once they fed themselves. And yes, they must certainly be rescued from progress, development, and relief programs.

But they must not be changed. Above all else, they simply must not be changed.

CHAPTER TWO

How the Lushest Land in the World Fell Prey to Famine

When you say the word *famine,* most people immediately think of a specific occurrence. For those in the "business" of fighting hunger, that famine will most likely be one they worked on—one they studied and analyzed, or perhaps one for which they were members of the relief effort. But for most of us, the image that jumps to mind will be a famine that had a special significance for our specific generation—one that occurred and received great attention during our point in history.

For many Americans, that means the famine in Bangladesh. The terrible suffering that prompted former Beatle George Harrison to stage "The Concert for Bangladesh" was a forerunner of the LiveAid events and perhaps the first major attempt by a popular musician to tackle world hunger. Harrison's efforts did quite a bit to raise people's consciousness about the devastation that famine can cause. And the heart-breaking pictures he showed—even on the cover of the fund-raising album that was released—set the standard for the kind of visual impact that is still used to get people's attention. The music created at that concert and the images associated with the whole event ensured that *Bangladesh* would become synonymous with *famine* for many people.

Younger people today probably don't think of Bangladesh, however. For them, *famine* is synonymous with the barrage of disturbing images that were shown between the musical offerings during the mammoth day-long LiveAid fund-raising effort organized by Bob Geldof in 1985.

And in the case of Africa, the ironic comparison with past abundance is even more striking than with Bangladesh. I was just reading a report on a wonderful type of wild grass that has great potential to halt erosion—the washing away of topsoil, which is a root cause of much famine—in areas with fragile soils and few trees. As a graphic example of the tragedy that something as innocent-sounding as erosion can cause, the report referred to Africa's lost glory: "Topsoil losses can be so devastating that in the past they have brought down whole civilizations. North Africa, for example, was once the granary and 'woodlot' of the Roman Empire" (National Academy of Sciences, National Research Council, *Vetiver Grass,* 1989).

Yes, Africa was once so lush, so green, so overwhelmingly productive that it was literally the farm of the most impressive empire the world has seen to date. Africa was so full of life that—many anthropologists and archeologists now agree—the continent was the actual place of origin of human beings. At the very least, there is more evidence placing the first of our recognizable ancestors there than anywhere else on the globe.

But you don't have to go back millennia to find such a different Africa. There are people alive today who remember a continent very different than the way it is now. In 1985, a U.S. Congress subcommittee held hearings designed to garner support for sustainable agriculture in Africa.* ("Sustainable agriculture" simply means growing food with local resources instead of with expensive imported items such as chemical fertilizers and pesticides.) As we reviewed the 900-plus pages of testimony, we were struck by the similarity of many people's observations of how much Africa had changed in just the last thirty or forty years. Or less. In fact, Tim Valentine, a representative to Congress from North Carolina, and a member of the subcommittee, opened a session by reminding all present that "Twenty years ago Africa was self-sufficient in producing food to feed its people."

The group *Africa Tomorrow* presented especially striking testimony about the changes that have occurred. (This group includes such varied individuals as actor Ed Asner, ventriloquist and doctor Paul Winchell [he not only entertains millions with his wonderful characters, but has saved many lives with his highly regarded medical inventions], and Henry J. Heimlich, M.D., the physician whose world-famous emergency procedure for choking victims has saved countless lives.) They began with the frightening statistic that in the Sahel—a vast and extremely fragile portion of Africa that includes Ethiopia, Nigeria, and the Sudan—5 million hectares (a hectare equals about 2.5 acres) have been lost to the desert in the last fifty years. Think of it! Over 12 million acres of land—land that could have grown food, if intelligently managed—turned to dust. Since 1940. During the lifetime of many of us.

As recently as twenty or thirty years ago, Africa was much greener than today. You hear stories from the old hands, the people who worked in Africa when they were in their teens and twenties, and who are now in their fifties and sixties. These "old hands" point

---

*Reported in *Prospects for Sustainable Development in SubSaharan Africa,* a report prepared by the Subcommittee on Natural Resources, Agriculture Research, and Environment, of the Committee on Science, Space, and Technology, House of Representatives, for 99th Congress, 1st Session, 1985, published in 1987.

to areas of desert and barren hillsides, and tell you of lush grasslands and fertile mountains that used to be. Of majestic wild animals that used to roam and hunt, enriching the land beyond
description with their grace and beauty.

I met one of those men in Ethiopia, in 1985, the year after the last
really big famine there. His name is John McMillan, and he was
working for the organization *WorldVision* at the time. In 1985 he
was about sixty-five years old, and had been in Ethiopia forty-five
years ago. He went there as a teenager right after World War II.
The very area where we met was a place in which he had spent a
considerable amount of time four decades previously. He pointed
to a treeless hillside.

"When I was here in the '40s that hillside was covered with
trees," he told me. "And there were lions," he said with the sadness
of a man who may have been a bit afraid of the great cats then, but
missed their roars and majesty now. Listening to his voice, you
could imagine a female lion bringing down a gazelle in the tall
grass while the green mountains shimmered in the distance. You
could see an abundance of life.

"It was the breadbasket of Africa," he said. Now, remember, he's
talking about Ethiopia. A name much more likely to bring to mind
images of starving children and barren wastelands—not lush
mountains and lions lounging in the sun.

"Mussolini marched in here for a reason," he reminded me. Like
the Roman conquerors centuries before, the Axis powers saw the
tremendous agricultural potential of Africa. They saw a farm the
size of a continent that could feed the millions of soldiers fighting
their awful war.

"And that lushness was typical of Africa at the time. It wasn't
just this area," my friend explained. "Africa was full of trees and all
kinds of animals.

"All gone now," he added, with a sad shake of his head. "All gone
now."

So what happened? Even though it's a mistake to try to talk about "Africa" as if that immense continent were one simple place (just the area consistently affected by drought is three times the size of the United States), you can safely say that as recently as a hundred years ago traditional methods of farming were the norm.

Because Africa is so large and so radically different from place to place, those traditional methods took many forms. The kind of system that worked well on a lush hillside or near a river delta would be very different from farming that was successful in an area where local water is virtually nonexistent and rains are scarce, for example.

But no matter where they were practiced, those traditional forms of farming did have several things in common. One is that the people farming these different types of land all grew a mixture—a wide variety—of crops. It would have been unthinkable to simply plant massive amounts of one crop (not to mention nutritionally dangerous, and pretty boring at mealtime). Everyone grew variety—a mixture of grains, tubers, and fruits, as well as green plants and other crops that sometimes supplied food and at other times supplied the ingredients for local medicines.

Another common element is that most African farmers also practiced a system of rotation. After a piece of land had been used for a few years, it would be pretty well drained of its natural nutrients (this is especially true in the tropics, where the soil is much less rich than you might think). Typically, the farmers either burned the fields or simply moved to another area for a while. Or both. Years later, after the land had rested and regenerated itself, they or someone else would return and farm that space again. Basically, their natural instincts led them to develop a fallow system— much like the government still pays some American farmers to follow—that protected the land and ensured good harvests.

Then the Europeans arrived. We know all too well that initially they farmed the people themselves—abducting the African natives and selling into slavery those that survived the hellish journey across the ocean. But it didn't end there. Unfortunately, history doesn't pay as much attention to the second incursion of the Europeans. After the human slave trade dried up, the Europeans enslaved the land itself.

They saw Africa as a place to be conquered, colonized, and managed. They saw tremendous areas of lush land—land whose potential, they felt, was being wasted by primitive people with primitive cultures and (to European eyes) primitive methods of agriculture. Colonized, Africa's land created tremendous wealth for the Europeans. But the manner in which they used that land set in motion a chain of events that has contributed to the problems the continent faces today.

For one thing, the Europeans brought corn to Africa. And, unfortunately, corn grew very well there. I say, "unfortunately," because Africa today would be much better off if the land hadn't been so well suited to corn. Maybe the Europeans would have given up and gone off and abused someone else's land. Maybe they would have used Africa's land in a less destructive manner. But the corn grew well, and so they stayed. And the massive amounts of corn they grew—again, we're talking about a lusher, much more productive Africa back then—had two basic effects that helped lead to the problems of today.

Too much corn leads to too many people. Here in America we also grow a lot of corn. We eat some of that corn, but a huge proportion of the harvest goes to feed animals.

That's not the case in Africa. Throughout most of the central part of the continent, you find the tsetse fly, which likes to bite cattle on the back of the neck. The cattle get sleeping sickness and die. Oddly enough, people can manage there better than cattle. And so, there have always been vast amounts of land, much of which was extremely fertile, which could be farmed, but couldn't be used for livestock, or even to grow food for livestock.

So corn was grown. And people ate the corn. Over the years African people have become accustomed to growing and eating a type of corn that is very different from anything that most Americans have ever seen. It's a white corn, not yellow. But it's not the kind of supersweet white corn—like Silver Queen—that we eat in the summer. It's a white field corn that is not picked fresh, but left out on the stalk until it dries and hardens. After picking, the people grind it up into cornmeal and eat it in a number of ways.

It is delicious, by the way. I love to eat this corn. In fact, I try to keep a steady supply around, and I make all my corn bread from white field corn. Like Africans, I just choose not to eat yellow cornmeal. The yellow is considered more nutritious, but the white has a powerful, wonderful flavor in the mouth.

So a tremendous amount of corn was—and still is—grown. But most of the corn was not grown for export. The European colonizers—and, more recently, the development experts—had long-range, far-reaching plans. They knew that Africa could produce a huge amount of coffee, cocoa, sisal, citrus, palm tree products like coconuts and palm oil, and expensive nuts like cashews. Those were products for which there was a good cash market in the West. And they also required a lot of cheap labor to produce.

So the colonizers set out to "fatten up" the people. They fed them lots of corn and introduced the concept of Western-style public health so that there would be lots of locals to work the vast plantations of cash crops. Of course, some of the public health improvements, especially the more recent ones, were done for humanitarian reasons as well as fiscal, but the result was the same: Because of the abundance of corn and the improvements in health care, the population soared.

Now, obviously, no one is going to say that health care improvements such as better sanitation and infant vaccination shouldn't have been introduced to Africa. In fact, the increase in population caused by those improvements in public health doesn't seem to have been the real problem.

Most experts feel that Africa's own natural resources could have handled the population increase that was the natural—but totally unforeseen—result of introducing modern medicine. *If* the change had been limited to medicine and public health improvements alone. But it wasn't. There was more food as well. More food and better medicine meant more people were being born, and more of those people were surviving. Which meant more food was necessary. And, of course, more food meant more people. . . .

Initially, it didn't seem like a bad strategy. And when some people finally did become concerned that there were no longer any natural checks on the population level, their solution, unfortunately, was simply to grow more corn.

But the corn was doing several things to the land that would soon make that solution impossible. If you've ever grown corn, either on a farm or in your garden, you know what a hungry plant we're talking about. Corn devours nutrients. You have two choices with corn: Feed it vast amounts of fertilizer or plant in a different place every season. So the first, and simplest effect of all this corn was to rapidly suck the land dry. Corn is not user friendly—the plant has a huge appetite and doesn't give very much back to the soil after the harvest.

In fact, under most circumstances, corn isn't even cost effective. It's very difficult to get enough money back from the ear or two that a plant produces to justify the fertilizer that you put into growing those ears. (That's why corn production almost everywhere has to be subsidized to some degree by governments. And even with those subsidies, a farmer will never get rich growing corn.)

In the development plans that were drawn up in the 1960s and 1970s to address the problem of out-of-control population growth in many Third World countries, massive amounts of fertilizer were shipped into Africa (and other developing nations) from overseas—at enormous cost, of course. This fertilizer—all chemical based, mostly derived from petroleum—didn't do anything to improve the soil, but it did keep the corn growing.

Before the fertilizer arrived, and in areas it never reached, the fields were burned and abandoned after each harvest. Again, with a manageable population, such a method might work. If you were lucky and conditions were right and local plants popped up quickly to keep the soil in place, and you let the fields regenerate for a decade or so, you could probably grow another corn crop there.

But as the population grew, long fallow periods became impossible. People tried to use the land again much too quickly. And, of course, a farmer—anywhere—should never count on being lucky. Right after the harvest—especially if the field is burned—the land is in great danger. Because there are no longer any plants in the soil to keep that soil in place. All it takes is a hard rain or a strong wind and that soil is gone.

And the more land that's exposed at any one time, the worse the problem becomes. For unless a driving rain is broken down by plants—trees are the best choice—those seasonal torrents of tropical water are not absorbed by the soil. Instead, those rains wash away soil with incredible efficiency.

Soil not held tight in the ground by roots is also at the mercy of the wind. And Africa is home to the kind of merciless, legendary winds that they name fast cars after (the scirocco, for example).

No wonder the soil losses in Africa are so staggering. (As are the losses in America, by the way. Many areas in the United States can now only grow food by using enormous amounts of chemicals. There's simply no soil left—just enough little bits of pulverized rock and sand to hold the crop roots in place. And that's why famine is such a distinct possibility in America as well as in the Third World.)

Slowly, over the course of the last hundred years, huge tracts of ecologically sound land in Africa have been cleared, used for a couple of years, abandoned, and then claimed by the desert. Thousands of native plants and millions of acres of grasslands were lost. Millions of trees were cut down. All so that vast stands of corn and cash crops could be planted.

Those crops not only left the land helpless after their harvest, but also stripped the land of all the nutrients that the fragile tropical soil had built up over millions of years of natural cycles of death, decay, and then regeneration.

But because Africa was so lush when all this started, and because Africa is so vast, the process was able to go on for a century before being crushed under the weight of its own foolishness. Lots of corn was grown. The population exploded in response to this enormous increase in the food supply. Slowly, at the same time, the same corn was also causing the land to become less and less productive.

In retrospect, it's hard not to have seen famine coming. It was inevitable—just a matter of time.

But the real problem is wood. Africa was "Rome's woodlot." Wherever did it all go?

Some of those trees— most of them—were cleared for agriculture, with the result that we just discussed. Sadly, no lesson has been learned, it seems. In other parts of the world, right now forests worth billions are being cut and torched in order that cattle can graze (for a surprisingly short period of time, it turns out) so that we can eat cheap hamburgers at fast food restaurants.
Unimaginable numbers of fabulous, spectacular forms of life of all kinds are being wiped out. Animals, reptiles, plants, and microscopic creatures found nowhere else in the world are being made extinct before we can find them, study them, analyze them. Before anyone can examine them in the ongoing search for new medical discoveries based on nature; the cures we're all desperately hoping science will provide. But those discoveries—those

cures—can never come because we're selling off the natural laboratory at flea market prices! Sorry about that endangered tree frog with the promising venom that might have reversed rheumatoid arthritis. Oops, looks like we lost this rare tropical orchid with that strange pigment that might have had the potential to treat cancer.

Here, have a burger instead.

Sorry. I guess I'm off on a tangent again, talking about the destruction of the tropical rain forests when I should be presenting my plan for famine prevention—of which trees are an integral part. But it's a tangent worth going off on. The misery already caused by the destruction of trees in Africa is so overwhelmingly obvious. How can the same shortsighted actions be beginning anew in another lush part of the world? I realize that human greed is immense, but doesn't it have *any* limits? Have we as a species lost our basic sense of self-preservation? The horror that tree cutting has caused in Africa is a lesson in history that we should choose not to repeat in the gloriously beautiful rain forests of Brazil and elsewhere.

In Africa, at least the reasons were better. The felling of trees in Africa, although harmful, at least made some sense. More sense than in the rain forests, where the felling is prompted by a totally flawed economic incentive.

The most obvious economic flaw, of course, is that the natural wonders—the wildlife, the plants, the unique micro-organisms with their unknown but potentially strong benefit to science, the stunningly beautiful ecological system itself is easily worth much more than anyone will ever make from the raw timber or the beef.

But that's not the flaw I'm referring to. Some people see the beauty and medical-scientific potential of the rain forests as theoretical. Some even see the protective benefits to our ozone layer and the forestalling of the greenhouse effect as "theoretical." What I'm talking about is that the tree-felling enterprise is flawed even from the purely business point of view.

Flawed, because, as we said earlier, tropical soils can be surprisingly infertile. All the nutrients the tropical soil has to offer are actually in those massive, beautiful trees. If the trees were to fall naturally and rot away over a period of years, they would return those nutrients to the earth. But when the trees come crashing down and are hauled away, so are the nutrients. The land left behind isn't good for much—it's practically sterile—and grazing cattle quickly turn it into a wasteland. Since the plan doesn't work (and because the people behind the plan won't acknowledge their basic error), the saws must roar on to clear more land even faster. What they leave behind is destined to quickly become a virtual desert.

In a small but excellent book entitled *To Feed the Earth,* the World Resources Institute (WRI) makes this same point that tropical forests are very different from ours: "Cut a temperate-zone forest and 97% of the nutrients available for new growth will remain in the soil. Cut a tropical forest and almost all of these nutrients will be hauled away in the timber."

In Africa, corn kills trees. Many trees have been felled specifically to clear land to grow corn. But most have not. Most have been cut for a different reason. But surprisingly, corn is still a factor in the death of those trees as well. Even those trees that weren't cleared for corn or cash crop production were felled indirectly by the corn. They were cut not to grow corn, but by those whom the corn grew, so to speak.

As the population expanded rapidly, the enormous numbers of people needed much more wood than had ever been required in the past. Wood is, by most accounts, still the only source of fuel for between 75 and 90 percent of rural Africans. They are the people who have made the hillsides treeless. They don't cut down trees for the fun of it; they do it because they need the fuel. They need wood for cooking and for the fires that kill the bugs in their roofs and impart a sense of serenity and warmth to their lives.

But the effects of too many people cutting too many trees have been devastating—not only to the land, but to the people themselves. As I mentioned earlier, trees are one of the best ways to ensure that the infrequent deluges of rainwater are absorbed into the ground. Trees help keep soil where it is—especially on hillsides, where, without trees, Africa's heavy seasonal rains practically strip-mine the mountains of their rich soil.

You can see it when you drive from Dar es Salaam to Negril. About halfway along the 80-mile drive you encounter a very fertile ridge running toward Negril. When you first notice it, it is full of trees. Not many people live in the area. But as you get closer to Negril the trees begin to thin out. When you finally get within 10 or 20 miles, the ridge is bare. There are no trees. It is a very impressive thing to see—this ridge—in both its forested and barren states.

And the population of Negril is expanding rapidly. There are approximately 200,000 people there now, and that figure is expected to reach 300,000 in another five years. Those people are just going to walk further and further to get that wood. You can see them now, gathering wood enormous distances from their homes because they've exhausted the supply within a day or two's carrying distance.

The people must use more and more of their personal energy—their nutritional reserves—every time they go out to gather wood. The time that should be spent growing food is spent instead on the ever-lengthening walk for wood. And the land from which the wood is taken becomes barren and lifeless—claimed by the ever-growing miles of desert.

———

And women are doing that carrying. Because of their special importance in the Third World, we're going to devote an entire chapter to women later in the book. But I'd like to point out now that the people our famine prevention plan is truly designed to help are women.

Women do the farming. They collect the firewood. And, of course, they are the ones most burdened by the population problem as well. On this matter there is literally no disagreement whatsoever. Experts agree that women perform about 90 percent of the farming and wood gathering in the Third World.

As many people (at least the ones who are paying attention) have said when addressing these issues, any solutions to the problems of hunger, famine, firewood, and population in the Third World have to be solutions that work for women. It is the women who must walk hours, sometimes days, before they reach a stand of wood they can use. Of course, they can only carry so much back, so it becomes a terrible cycle of wasted energy and time. There are many instances of families becoming malnourished despite stocks of food on hand—simply because the women were too exhausted to prepare and cook that food after the farming and wood collection was finally done for the day.

It's a terrible burden for women, and one that famine relief programs simply don't address. Although it may be hard for many of us to understand—especially since the messages with which we are bombarded stress the constant need for food and medicine—the firewood crisis is a bigger problem in Africa than lack of food. Even the traditional development experts, the ones who have actually caused or compounded many of the current difficulties— agree that the firewood problem is the most serious.

Luckily, things aren't as bleak as they seem. A solution to the firewood crisis (actually the re-emergence of a technique Africans themselves used centuries ago) is at the core of our famine prevention proposal. Unlike the usual development plans, our solution doesn't involve improved stoves that the people don't want or fuels that Africans can't afford. Rather, it's a system that allows even the smallest landholders to grow the wood they need *as* they farm.

Our solution ends the dusty, endless march of the Third World women. It stops the strip-mining of the hillsides' fertility. And, rather than simply growing trees in space that would otherwise grow food, our plan grows trees whose presence actually *enhances* food production.

The technique is a real bright point, a beacon of hope. I'm a little ahead of myself in mentioning it, but I'm afraid that if I just dwell on the problems, things might begin to seem overwhelming. The seemingly endless negative side effects of colonialism and development presented to you one after another might seem too much to bear. Certainly too much to begin to reverse. You might just want to give up.

But please don't. I believe that it's essential that we first must understand the problems if we're going to take steps that really have the potential to begin to alleviate this incredible suffering. We *must* understand the mistakes of the past. That is essential. If we do not, we risk repeating those errors. And then, like the well-intentioned proponents of 1960s- and 1970s-style development, we could take a bad situation and, by honestly trying to help, make it even worse.

So if you need to see a solution now—something to fill you with hope and brighten your spirits—skip ahead to Chapter 8, where I explain the incredible successes that people have achieved with the technique called *alley cropping*.

No, alley cropping is not a plan whereby people grow food in the narrow back streets behind buildings in the cities. It's a farming method that capitalizes on the growing of trees and plants together in the same space; the plants growing in "alleys" between rows of trees.

Wonderful trees. Marvelous trees that provide free fertilizer, animal food—even food for humans (see Chapter 5). And, of course, firewood.

But after you read Chapter 8, come on back. The next chapter in this section finishes explaining the problems that have led to so many people living under the shadow of famine, and it may be the most important chapter of all. It's about reversing vulnerabilities. If you want to be stronger—as a person or a nation—you need to know and understand your weaknesses. You need to know where you're vulnerable to attack, so you can concentrate on building up that area first. And if you want to help someone else protect themself, you need to know and understand the vulnerabilities that leave that person open to danger.

As I said, this listing of the vulnerabilities that people at risk of famine need to reverse may be the most important part of this section. I need you to read it. I need you to understand it. And that's because I expect—I know—that many of you are going to think of ways to improve our plan. Some of you may even come up with something that never occurred to us, but something, nevertheless, that will be perfectly applicable to some of the situations that breed famine.

As I was talking to my editor early on, I said, "I don't want people to be limited by my suggestions, by what the Rodale Institute and others have already accomplished in the Third World." I said that I expected that some of you out there would have great ideas to complement—or even replace—my own, and that I didn't want to do anything to limit or discourage those ideas. "Someone out there could have an idea that might save thousands of lives," I said. "Someone else might have an idea that's fabulous, but that would only work in one small area. Maybe that idea would only affect a few people in that small area.

"Maybe it's an idea that will only save three lives. But think of that," I said. "When's the last time you had a chance to save three lives?"

This next chapter contains the basic ground rules for our efforts, describing those vulnerabilities that must be reversed if we are to stop famine before it gains a foothold. By truly understanding what it is we are up against, perhaps *you* can save three lives. Maybe many, many more.

CHAPTER THREE

How Foreign Aid Has Only Increased the Vulnerability of Hungry People

This is the chapter my editor didn't want me to do. I originally wanted to call it "the failures of development." When he first heard that expression, he rolled his eyes up toward the ceiling and made a gesture with his hands like a bird's wings.

"What's that?" I asked, puzzled.

"Your readers, flying away in droves," he said. Then he pointed to the mound of books we had collected on famine, hunger, and the problems with relief programs, foreign aid, and development. Many were good books that made strong points and suggested good future directions.

Unfortunately, few—if any—of those well-intentioned works have ever been read by anyone other than university researchers. We call them "shelf books." Thoughtfully and carefully written, they were published, achieved their place of honor on shelves in a couple of hundred libraries, and then were forgotten. They are desperately lonely books, and we were determined that this book not join them in that kind of isolation. This chapter in particular, feared my editor, could well turn our good intentions into just another shelf book.

But, as I said before, it's crucial that we understand what went before if we're to really change things. There are points that must be made about famine relief programs, foreign aid, and—most of all—the failures of development, if we are not to repeat decades of mistakes.

So please, stay with me here. I'd hate to wind up on a shelf.

The reason so many books on this vital subject do wind up gathering library dust is that the problem is often more complex than most people realize.

Often there *is* food available during a famine—or crops are grown that are either destined for export or are inedible, or both.

Here's a brief excerpt from an article that recently appeared in a medical journal that makes some excellent points and ends with the most horrifying examples of poor choices that I have ever encountered:

> The genesis of the problem of food production and nutrition of African, Asian and Central and South American countries can be traced back to the beginning of "inter-continental trade" and the emergence of colonialism. Local food patterns and social and economic orders that had evolved to benefit the inhabitants and the environment were destroyed. . . .
>
> At present . . . famine is always present under the surface. . . .
>
> A large proportion of fertile land in the developing countries is used for the production of cash crops. . . . In Ethiopia, in spite of

chronic famine the proportion of land designated for cash-crop production has progressively increased in the last twenty years.

Similarly, in the Sudan, the majority of the inhabitants suffer from eternal undernutrition; yet in the Geizera irrigation project, which is the largest agricultural scheme in Sub-Sahara Africa, cotton and groundnuts are grown for export.

The Sahelian countries which are often associated with starvation and recurrent drought are net exporters of agricultural commodities—mostly cotton and peanuts. Although Kenya has one of the highest rates of malnutrition it exports coffee, tea, cotton and, even more surprisingly, flowers such as carnations that are grown by the side of Lake Naivasha. (K. Ghebremeskel, "The State of Food Production and Nutrition in the Developing Countries," *Nutrition and Health, 6,* 1989)

Carnations! If the notion weren't so horrifying, so blindingly awful, it could almost be humorous. How could this be? A nation where hunger rules with a hard, heavy hand—growing flowers instead of food?

The author of the article, a member of the London Zoological Society, provides some answers to that question. Answers that are—unfortunately—already too well known by many of us who have grappled with the hunger issue.

One is foreign debt. Cash crops (meaning food grown exclusively for export) are considered essential by governments who care more about meeting the massive interest payments on their foreign debt than about feeding their people. Often, a nation's best land is used for something as seemingly senseless as flower growing, while peasant farmers try to grow food for their families on sand and rocks.

Another reason is that some fairly idiotic ideas have been hatched, proposed, accepted, and then implemented in the context of foreign aid and development. (By the way, I'm sorry to use such harsh words when discussing something as well meaning as development, but I just can't talk about it any other way. The vast majority of what has occurred under the banner of development has had a strongly negative impact on the people the projects in question were supposed to help. It's unfortunate, but if you live in the Third World and are unlucky enough to be graced with development, it's likely that you will end up much worse off than you were before.)

But back to growing flowers instead of food. I'm not familiar with the carnation project personally, but I wouldn't be surprised if development funds were used, and that, when originally proposed, the end result of this abomination was somehow predicted to be a great benefit to the local people.

Of course, you don't have to be a scientific genius to see the absurdity of using the best land in the region to cultivate lush fields of flowers while all around is the human misery caused by malnutrition. The sheer senselessness and inhumanity of the plan practically screams out at you.

In fact, it is only the scientific experts—the development planners, the aid approvers—who aren't able to see these incongruities. An objective look at the absurd and ecologically frightful schemes concocted in the name of development over the last few decades indicates that **only** those scientists are so blinded. But how can this be? Again, the author of the article that mentions the carnation farm explains—this time in a single sentence—how such degreed (and therefore seemingly intelligent) people can allow and often cause such things to occur: "It appears that the organizations [involved] are too bureaucratic and detached to realize that a good many of their programmes are of no consequence to the starving majority."

I agree, except that I would amend that last line. It's not simply that these programs are of no consequence; they are all too often of *negative* consequence. Growing carnations on the lushest land in a starving nation is not benign. It is not even neutral. The carnation plan does more than simply not feed people; it starves them. It increases, rather than reduces, their vulnerability.

The project wastes precious land that, properly managed, could feed thousands. And it sends a terribly wrong message about priorities, about the way that land—and people's lives—should be spent. That's the big revelation about the way foreign aid and development funds are used—not simply the scandalous fact that most international foreign aid money goes to military uses. Not the reality that much of the rest is wasted on huge projects (dams are a big favorite) that are totally inappropriate to the needs of the people.

No, the mind-boggling conclusion that you simply have to draw after examining project after project is that even the small percentage of foreign aid that does go toward plans to ease hunger is often spent in ways that leave those people much worse off than they were before the help arrived.

That's why our plan mandates that all money spent on development be spent small. As I have learned—and many other researchers have finally acknowledged—big plans don't work. In fact, they don't just not work—big plans have a distinct tendency to harm.

There's a wonderful fellow I know who's helping great things happen in Mexico right now. Believe it or not, he's a former IBM salesman who's now a rogue antidevelopment leader. I'd describe him more formally, but he has no title. If I tried to give him one, he'd probably get mad at me. In fact, because of all the harm that he and his colleagues have seen big organizations do, they even refuse to name the group that is currently doing so much to help the Mexican peasants become self-sufficient once again. Actually, it does have a name of sorts, but not the type we're used to hearing. Certainly not the kind with a bunch of capital letter initials frequently used to spell out something clever.

The group through which I know him best is known as a "hammock." That's because, he explains, the group, like a hammock, is flexible. The group supports people and makes them comfortable by fitting their needs. It assumes their shape when they get into it instead of forcing them to adapt to its shape. I know, it sounds pretty Zen-ish, but this hammock is a great example of an organization that really does help people in a developing country. And I believe this success is due largely to the fact that the people aren't forced to do things according to a foreign plan or shape. (In contrast, the big, foreign organizations often harm the people by doing just that—making them do something completely unnatural to their land and culture.)

It's a wonderful image, if you think about it. Would you rather climb up into a nicely supportive hammock that holds you softly and comfortably, spreading your body weight over a large area? Or would you prefer your only choice to be a hard, straight-backed chair—seemingly designed to force your body into an unnatural position that puts a lot of painful strain on your lower back?

Anyway, this man's name is Gustavo Estava, and he recently told me how, in Mexico, the word *development,* when used at all, is used mostly as the butt of some very black-humor jokes by the peasants. This attitude actually prevails in most of the world. An old joke, familiar to farmers across the globe with minor changes depending on the crop mentioned, goes like this:

Extension agent: "Doesn't look like you're going to get any apples off that tree this year."

Farmer: "You're right. That's a peach tree."

Thanks to such lack of appropriate local knowledge and a tendency toward destructive techniques, "for a long time now, development has been recognized as a threat by the Mexican peasant," Estava explained.

"Most are aware that it has not only failed to help them, but it has undermined their reliance on the successful, centuries-old method of growing a diversity of crops."

For him, the failure of development is not theory. The negative results of those plans that were originally designed to help people are not mere opinion. As an example, he cited something fascinating that occurred when the Mexican oil boom went bust in the early 1980s:

> The Rural Development Bank of Mexico had come up with a plan that had literally forced the peasants to plant huge amounts of sorghum as animal feed. But in 1982, when the oil money ran out, the Bank ran short and the program failed.
>
> Without the Bank forcing them to plant sorghum, the peasants returned to their traditional style of agriculture, which was an intercropping of corn and beans. The immediate result was an improvement in the nutritional levels of the people.
>
> And the long-term result was the return of political power to the village.

That last part is far from unimportant. Often, development operations do more than just disrupt the agricultural scheme of an area. The invasion of a large group of experts with their big plans for big dams and big plantations often changes the local balance of power that's been in place for centuries.

How is the hammock approach different? I'll let Gustavo explain how it works:

> Instead of rules of access, we have trust and friendship. The hammock [has] a fund of around half a million dollars to support peasant projects or initiatives and for emergencies.
>
> Any morning a peasant group can come to the fund's offices asking for credit. [If money is available,] no more than two hours later they get the cheque.

If the fund is depleted, they are informed of the date they may return, estimated by the payment of [previous] money lent.

The operation takes the form of a donation in two ways; the fund donates to the peasant and the peasant in turn donates to the fund when the money is repaid. The people are simply told that the fund was created to support peasant groups and that it is maintained through the recovery of the credit granted

After five years of operation, the original fund has revolved four times, recovering more than 95 percent of the credit granted.

No peasant has refused to pay back. The outstanding 5 percent corresponds to groups confronting especially tough circumstances. The fund, of course, is not pressing them.

To many observers, to build on trust and friendship looks like a utopian, romantic fantasy [that] cannot operate in the real economic world. In contrast, these foundations are not only sound as a survival strategy, but also define a joyful, promising and fully pragmatic way of life.

[For peasants] to hang their livelihood on the promise of development or to be dependent on market forces or public institutions to make a living seems to be not only a foolish fantasy, but a dead end.

The list of success stories made possible by this seemingly small enterprise is truly enviable. As Gustavo explains,

The hammock [has been] used by its friends:
   • To improve corn cultivation practices
   • To examine the impact of fertilizers and pesticides on land and people and to experiment and use alternative practices, like those of organic agriculture
   • To install latrines, using original technologies, in urban and rural settlements
   • To disseminate techniques, for the construction of ovens in rural areas, that care both for the forest and women's dignity
   • To finance small peasant projects or the return of peasants from the cities to the countryside

- To collect old traditional musical instruments and songs and to play them for audiences in rural and urban areas
- To rescue forest land for its original peasant owners and to organize and implement the ecological and productive use of forests and wood
- To organize and implement practices against soil erosion and deforestation
- To experiment and implement alternative practices for intercropping and crop diversification
- To test, improve, and disseminate the use of medicinal plants
- To technically and politically support the work of traditional midwives
- To complement local knowledge and practices of healing with doctors' advice
- To test and disseminate practices for backyard farms
- To struggle for human rights
- To organize cooperatives
- To improve the collective use and care of the water

The list goes on and on. As Gustavo explains, "I could fill one hundred pages. [This] arbitrary selection of examples only offers a glance at our hammock's world." And I, in turn, only used about half of even that abbreviated list! Truly a massive number of worthwhile, sustainable, undeniably positive efforts funded with what would have to be considered a pittance by development standards. And a pittance that constantly replenishes itself in the form of donations back to the group that originally donated to those efforts! An example to us all of how things can—and should—be done to improve people's lives while reinforcing, not destroying, their culture. The hammock has even managed to make finance joyful!

One last thing before we swing ourselves out of the hammock. I think Gustavo would be angry if I fail to mention a fine point about the terminology of the hammock. As he explains, the group isn't supposed to be thought of as a hammock in itself. Rather, he prefers to say that the members of the group *have* a hammock. The difference is very important to him. The hammock doesn't belong to anyone. It's there to be used by anyone who knows (or even wants to learn) how to lie down in it correctly. And that, of course, could be just about anyone willing to give up the so-called luxury of the alternative—the Western-style, hard-backed, unyielding, lower-back-pain-inducing chair.

Nothing more typifies the rigid "chair" of Western-style agricultural development than the unfortunately named Green Revolution. I really wish they had called the Green Revolution something else—because it *sounds* so positive. The word *green* has a wonderful ring—a positive, ecological air to it.

The word is certainly used correctly by Greenpeace—the ecological freedom fighters who are among the many groups fighting to save the planet. And "buying green" in Europe—and slowly in North America—has come to mean supporting ecologically sound principles of business, politics, and agriculture—choosing organically grown fruits and vegetables while rejecting excess, wasteful packaging, and destructive, polluting business practices.

But the Green Revolution is about as far away from those examples as you can get. In the Third World, this misappropriated word *green* stands for chemical farming at its most hideous extreme: insecticides, herbicides, and chemical fertilizer by the supertanker load, by the megaton, by the football-field-full. The Green Revolution—despite providing increased harvests in the short run—has caused tremendous long-term damage in the Third World. The destruction of the land and contamination of the local water supplies are well documented. But perhaps the biggest act of destruction is that the short-term successes of this revolution have done a lot to delay research and funding into a return to a more natural style of farming. Because up until a few years ago the Green Revolution was the poster boy of chemical farming—the overwhelming success story of Western-style development tactics.

A bit of Green Revolution background: To combat hunger in India and Asia, vast areas were planted with a scientifically bred single strain of super-rice that (perhaps due to its artificial nature) had a huge appetite for chemical fertilizer and a stronger-than-average need for pesticide to protect it against hungry insects.

Once those chemicals were applied in large amounts, the immediate effects were truly astonishing. Yields responded dramatically. Record increases in harvests were recorded. But as the World Resources Institute's book, *To Feed the Earth,* wisely points out, "Record crops produced at the expense of next year's or the next decade's soil resources are nothing to be proud of."

One failure of the Green Revolution is that by relying exclusively on chemical fertilizers it added nothing real to the soil. The should-have been-foreseen result? When the inevitable happened, when the programs funding these massive supplies of chemicals ended (or when the chemicals themselves became illegal or just too expensive to buy), the land was left in much worse shape than before the "revolution." Another inevitable long-term failure that should have been foreseen was the poisoning of water supplies by the huge amounts of chemicals necessary to grow artificially created crops under such unnatural conditions.

Perhaps these things *were* foreseen. Perhaps the end was felt to justify the means. Or perhaps the experts never thought to look toward the future, preferring instead to luxuriate in the comforting present of bountiful crops. What they failed to anticipate, however, was that their period of reward—their "window" of success—would be so brief. In terms of time, the chemically cradled process known as the Green Revolution has been more of a peephole than a window.

As the World Resources Institute (WRI) points out: "In the

Chiang Mai Valley [in Thailand], rice harvests averaged four tons per hectare in 1969 and rose to 6.4 tons by 1971 with fertilization and use of high-yielding varieties, but steadily declined to the 1969 levels by 1977. Perhaps more disturbing, yields became about twice as variable during that time." Six years is a pretty short time for a "revolution" to come unglued. And the high variability of the yields sends a pretty strong message in itself—you can practically hear the earth screaming out in confusion.

So there you, the farmer, are six years later: wasting huge amounts of hard-to-find money because of your greatly increased need for fertilizer, but not getting any more rice than you did before the experts came in. What an improvement. And even if the native people actually were to revolt and toss out this phony revolution, it would take many years to build up the land, to repair the damage that a decade of chemical farming has done to the soil.

As WRI points out, China—which made a big switch from natural to artificial farming in the 1970s—may be the biggest example of how chemical farming on a massive scale simply cannot produce for long. Of course, as with any such system, at first you have the initial success: "In six years," WRI reports, "the Chinese tripled the use of chemical fertilizers and production of fertilized crops increased by 50 percent."

And then you have the inevitable result: The breakdown, the failure. "Yet chemicals were not necessarily the heroes in this story," WRI continues. As a visiting delegation of Chinese scientists explains, "In the decade since the chemical agricultural program began, even greater amounts of chemicals are needed to keep productivity high. In some cases, productivity is slowly declining despite increasing [use of chemical fertilizer]. Problems of pollution and erosion are reportedly widespread."

One problem of superfertilization is that it breeds supervulnerability. Pesticide breeds superpests. Plantation farming just makes pests' life easier. The so-called development experts point to their endless seas of genetically engineered super-rice and say, "Just look at all that food!" Standing there next to them, I see those same endless fields of identical plants and think, "Just look at all that vulnerability!"

Yes, vulnerability. Vulnerability to one pest, to one disease. It's a given in agriculture that growing several types of plants close to each other confuses pests. Mixed plantings slow them down, preventing their spread by presenting them with natural borders.

But a single crop that goes on for miles? All you need is one enterprising type of insect or determined disease to catch on to this inviting situation and that crop killer could conceivably spread like a prairie fire, devastating everything in its path (a path conveniently built by human hands, no less). That's because, in such a foolish form of agriculture, everything is really just *one* thing. And that suits single-crop insects like corn borers just fine. Before plantation farming, these pests were present, but relatively under control. Typically, they would find a small stand of their preferred crop, settle in, and stop when they reached the edge of any part of that field.

Pests such as the borers, that are specific to corn, won't cross an acre of broccoli or beans in a healthy, mixed-planting system— even if there is corn on the other side of those less-tasty plants. So they stay where they are, content. Their population, with a limited food supply, remains under control.

Insects that eat a wide variety of plants, such as the army worm, don't like to cross open land. As long as open spaces surround the stand they occupy, they'll stay where their plants are. And, again, the limited amount of food controls their population naturally.

But give insects endless acres of corn or any other crop back-to-back and it's like building a superhighway, a free public transit system for pests. You couldn't make their spread any easier if you picked them up and hand-carried them from plant to plant!

That's also true of weeds, including a devastating one known as *Striga*. (In the south of Africa, where it grows, they call it "witch weed," but its Latin name is Striga.) It's the worst kind of weed you can imagine. It spreads underground. You can't wipe it out. It can't be stopped. It latches onto a crop from underneath and sucks the life out from below. So, once Striga gets into an area, you have really difficult problems farming that land.

Although this weed has probably always been there in Africa, for centuries it was limited to fairly small areas because it couldn't—or wouldn't—spread across the open land between plantings. But after plantation farming started, there were no longer any natural boundaries to halt its expansion.

Striga spreads like mad, creeping from row to row in these endless seas of corn and cotton easier than you or I can walk across a carpeted room. Many experts feel that the explosive expansion of Striga in Africa is one of the single worst side effects of the plantation system.

In *To Feed the Earth,* the World Resources Institute points out that in 1977, 2 million tons of Green Revolution rice were lost to a virus (called the *tungro*, if you're curious) in Indonesia. The kicker is that the specific rice that fell prey to the virus—a Green Revolution hybrid known as IR36—was specifically engineered to resist a quite different threat: a local pest known as the brown planthopper.

Rather than rely on proven environmental controls—including centuries-old, no-cost techniques such as planting a wide variety of crops—development experts continue to insist that the best way to protect the fragile, artificial crops they insist on growing is with environmentally damaging artificial methods. Their answer when disease wipes out untold tons of food because only a single, vulnerable strain was planted? "We'll replant those thousands of acres with a different strain that we've bred to resist that disease," they say proudly.

And, of course, then it's simply a matter of time until another unexpected occurrence wipes out that variety as well (a hard piece of reality that, unfortunately, does not enter into the thinking of such planners).

But the appearance of an opportunistic insect or disease is not an unexpected occurrence to people who are paying attention, and it shouldn't be to the experts, either. Over several millennia, traditional farmers have learned that insects and disease are to be expected.

Both insects and disease are extremely efficient. Whenever we grow huge amounts of food for ourselves, it's fairly certain that something else out there is going to see that bounty as food as well. In a real sense, food creates life. And often that life is serious competition for us. If, by some miracle, we were even able to create some new kind of food that no insect currently eats, you can bet it wouldn't be long before one simply evolved to feast on that food. And pesticides, at least to those who have eyes to see, are not the answer to this simple reality of the food chain.

First, there are very few true pesticides, in the sense that they harm only pests. Almost all these poisons are extremely effective humanicides as well. The World Resources Institute points out that "as many as 400,000 illnesses and 10,000 deaths may be caused by pesticides every year worldwide—most of them in the developing world."

And second, although those chemicals are as much of a danger to us as they are to pests, the insects are remarkably better at adapting to those poisons than we are.

But the prevailing mentality is still "We'll dominate, we'll kill them. If the poisons that we've got don't work, we'll just make stronger poisons." And, of course, the highly adaptable insects become resistant to the new poisons as well, while the people who live in the area often wind up being sickened or killed by these increasingly toxic chemicals. (As others have pointed out, since a lot of this food is grown for export, those stronger poisons often come back to haunt us personally as well.)

Let's take a closer look at the problem of resistance—the innate ability of insects to quickly develop a tolerance to chemical poisons. The WRI notes that "The continuing spread of resistance . . . raises questions about the future stability of chemical-based pest control in industrialized and developing countries alike." As an example, WRI cites the case of the diamondback moth, which, thanks to development, now threatens all cabbage production in Malaysia. The moth, they report, has become resistant "to virtually all available pesticides." The diamondback moth is, of course, not an isolated example. Just the opposite—many insects are making various pesticides obsolete at a startling rate of speed.

One reason why insects are such extremely successful creatures in this regard is that their short individual life spans allow them to quickly make changes in their genetic structure—changes that can only occur over generations and that would take us centuries. This basic difference allows them to develop tolerance to our agricultural poisons—the poisons that are an essential component of Green Revolution-type strategies—within a few years of their first exposure to that toxin. Those years, for them, can see the passing of dozens—perhaps hundreds, even thousands—of generations. Unfortunately, we can't adapt nearly as quickly. The pesticides that are harmless to the pests will remain deadly to us for centuries.

Moreover, "there is not here." I had always known that the tropics harbored more plant-threatening disease than our temperate areas of climate, but until I read WRI's *To Feed the Earth* carefully, I didn't realize just how lopsided this ratio of vulnerability was. As WRI explains, the differences are astronomical: In temperate growing zones, 15 separate diseases have been reported to attack sweet potato crops. In the tropics, there are 111.

Rice? Fifty-four diseases threaten harvests here. But 500 to 600 have been recorded there (so it was really just a matter of time before one of those hundreds upon hundreds of diseases zeroed in on those genetically weak fields in Indonesia).

Tomatoes? In your backyard, this favored summertime crop may have to resist as many as 32 different diseases. Move to the tropics, put the same plants in the ground, and now you're up against 278.

These are not isolated examples. The difference exists across the board. The lesson to be learned is that there is not here. You can't farm the Sudan or the Philippines as if they were slightly displaced pieces of Iowa.

Forget for a moment the culture and the poverty—the fact that the people involved can't afford that U.S. style of high-priced farming (tractors, fuel, pesticides, herbicides). The differences are even more basic than that. Tropical soils are different, fragile almost beyond belief. Because there are no seasonal freezes, crop-eating insects are more plentiful. The diseases that threaten growing plants are almost unbelievably more abundant. Water is often scarce; sometimes it's practically nonexistent. And, in most areas, there simply are no roads to truck all that expensive Green Revolution equipment in. And where roads do exist, they would have to be improved greatly before we would consider them to be in merely terrible shape.

There is not here. And that's the single biggest reason why massive plans ostensibly designed to feed the people have often failed, taking people who were living on the edge of famine and pushing them right into its jaws.

You simply can't send U.S. farming equipment and know-how to another part of the world where nothing even vaguely resembles the United States and expect the system to work. Luckily, I see more and more people in official positions acknowledging that now. But this enlightenment has been a terribly long time coming.

Many years will be needed to reverse the damage, but eventually the hard-working, fertilizer-producing water buffalo will return in sufficient numbers to replace the rusting skeletons of the diesel-guzzling, pollution-belching tractors that have died early deaths due to a lack of spare parts.

A small, fearful aside: The failures of the Green Revolution in Asia and India are becoming more and more apparent every day. One can only hope that those in power have the courage to admit their mistakes before this unnatural form of agriculture begets a true, international disaster.

What might appear if this foolish form of chemical farming doesn't stop? A new insect? Perhaps a mutant locust, impervious to our most toxic chemicals, but with a sinister twist—say five times the breeding capacity or reproductive speed of its already deadly natural cousin? Or will it be a new disease? One that takes root in this unnatural landscape, but quickly spreads—perhaps on the wind—to menace the rest of the world?

Previous famines may pale in comparison to the unknown horrors that could be unleashed.

Even though it's obvious that Green Revolution techniques could never work in Africa, people have tried to foster this bizarre concept in what was once the garden spot of the earth. Thank goodness, it never had a chance. Africa isn't Asia, and it isn't India. As Donald Curtis and the other authors of the British book *Preventing Famine* (1988) point out in their introduction, "The vast drought-prone areas of Africa are very different from the flat, irrigable or well-watered areas of the world where the 'green revolution' and other technologies have made their impact."

Again, even though Africa is the sum of many divergent parts, some things can be said about the continent as a whole. Africa is fragile. It also has great agricultural potential. The land fed vast numbers of people for millions of years before outside efforts simultaneously sabotaged its agricultural potential and artificially bolstered the population. Depending on how those in power now choose to treat its land, Africa could once again be green (a true and natural green, not the artificial green of the Green Revolution) or it could continue to turn brown. The color of the desert. Lifeless.

A vast area known collectively as sub-Saharan Africa is where those choices will have the biggest effect. It is here that people who make decisions about agriculture have a remarkable power to work for or against the desert. Lately, the people in power seem to have been virtually in the employ of the desert. The leaders have been very good to the sands, helping them reach out and spread their barren domain. Part of this sandy expansion has been achieved with the use of Green Revolution techniques: attempting to grow high-yield varieties of crops with heavy water requirements in arid lands. Again, anyone but a development expert could easily see the fault in such logic.

And yet the chronic lack of water—especially reliable water—is not the strongest point against the use of Western farming techniques in Africa. One of the strongest arguments against those techniques—and one of the strongest arguments for our own plan, our return to a very slightly modernized form of ancient agriculture—is Africa itself. The continent is simply not suited to the Green Revolution technique.

Consider the roads, for instance. Even if it made ecological sense to import those genetically engineered superplants and the chemicals and diesel-fueled equipment necessary to grow them, it simply can't be done, mostly because the roads just aren't there. Where there are roads, there are also soldiers, waiting to waylay such shipments (and relief convoys as well), kill the drivers, and steal the trucks and their contents. The chemicals, seeds, and equipment are then sold on the black market. Relief food goes to soldiers. Sometimes it is simply destroyed.

In Rwanda, WRI notes, "attempts to introduce Western-style agriculture to the region have failed, partly because the required [supplies] are so expensive but more because supplies are frequently interrupted." Rwanda, like a huge amount of Africa, is not only landlocked but surrounded by countries that are beset by every form of civil disturbance imaginable. And, while we all hope that Africa can somehow, someday find peace with itself, we cannot make plans based on that assumption. Not with hungry people depending on the realistic nature of our plans.

And even if (or I should say optimistically, when) peace comes to Africa, the roads will still be a question mark. I can't begin to tell you just how bad the roads are. Many roads were built as part of development projects, but were never maintained. Billions for construction but nothing for upkeep. Even the big-planning, big-spending developers acknowledge that the existing roads are now too far gone to be salvaged and that there's not enough money to build new ones. As Norman Gall, a Brazilian economist, reported in the *Wall Street Journal* a few years back, "over the past two decades, 85 countries lost $45 billion worth of roads." Not destroyed in wars. Simply rotted away because developers never considered the necessity of maintenance.

Gall sums up the picture by quoting a World Bank report: "The developing world's road building boom in the 1960s and 1970s created an infrastructure that has been crumbling in the 1980s and threatens to collapse in the 1990s." And that's the opinion of the organization that *built* many of those roads.

Besides, the vast majority of people in rural Africa—those who are most at risk of famine—don't live anywhere near a road. The seeds, supplies, chemicals, and equipment simply can't reach them.

And even if they could, the Green Revolution way still doesn't make the most important kind of sense—economic sense. Dollars and sense. It's just too expensive. Even if the system did work (which I don't believe it could—even in the short run—in Africa), it would soon collapse under the weight of flawed economics. Back in 1985 at a Washington, DC, hearing on sustainable agriculture, the administrator of the U.S. Agency for International Development (USAID, or AID) acknowledged that it cost more to get fertilizer from an African port to an African farm than it did to get the material to Africa in the first place.

But that doesn't mean things are hopeless. We simply need to realize that new solutions are necessary. Solutions different from the ones imposed on these poor people so far.

First, planting huge fields of single crops of corn, of rice, of cassava—of anything—invites disease and pestilence. It gives native weeds like Striga an invitation to spread as never before, virtually building a high-speed roadway for weed expansion.

Second, chemical dependency is expensive, ecologically poisonous, and extremely damaging to the most important factor in any farming situation—the soil itself.

Third, disrupting native cultures with foreign ideas manages to be culturally condescending, sexist (men telling women what to do) and racist all at the same time. That's quite an achievement for something that's being done under the guise of charity.

And fourth, the neglect—or outright eradication—of native species that is a natural by-product of the Green Revolution and plantation farming goes beyond the bounds of simple cruelty to people of another culture, another color. It's a kind of genocide that eradicates every trace of the people: their plants, their culture, and in the case of famine, their very lives.

Such an approach is wrong. And it doesn't even work.

CHAPTER FOUR

Famine Relief Is Not the Answer

The preceding chapter was the part of this book my editor feared the most. He was afraid it would be boring. Now comes the section *I* approach with the most caution, the most uncertainty. Not because I fear that it will bore you—just the opposite. My fear is not that I will lose your attention, but that I will get too much of your attention, and by doing so, be misunderstood. (Or that I will be understood perfectly and you will get angry at me nonetheless.)

The subject is something I touched on briefly in the first chapter. We see images of starving people on TV and in newspapers, magazines, and direct mail campaigns. And we give.

We *must* give. As caring human beings, we have no choice. Giving reinforces our humanity, making us more than we were. And yet *the relief efforts to which we give our money simply don't work*. Please don't misunderstand that statement. I have feared that you might misunderstand me on this point from the moment I decided to do this book.

Earlier on I mentioned how—intellectually, not emotionally—you have to understand that you cannot help the people in those pictures. Many are already dead by the time you see their image. And most of the rest are too far along the path of malnutrition to come back to anything but a painful, crippled life—even if your donated food could reach them in time.

You must realize intellectually that there is a time lapse involved. Typically, a year or more may elapse before donations can be translated into food that has been purchased, shipped, and finally delivered to the isolated areas where the starving people wait. In his scathing (and excellent) critique of relief programs, *The Politics of Food Aid* (1988), famine expert Lloyd Timberlake points out that most of the food sent to Ethiopia in response to the 1984 famine arrived 400 days after it was promised to be there. And Timberlake goes on to explain that the true time lag was actually much worse. He recounts that there were official warnings beginning in 1982 that food would soon be urgently needed. But nothing was done. More warnings; 1983 came and went; the drought got worse. More warnings; no food. The starvation marches began.

Early in 1984, in a last-ditch effort, Timberlake and a U.N. High Commissioner for Refugees separately took groups of journalists to the areas hardest hit to show them that millions were in danger of starvation. And then, he writes, finally "the televised footage of babies dying appeared in the world's living rooms in the autumn of 1984." Only then did the money begin to be raised, so that the food could finally arrive in 1985. Three years after the drought began.

The food arrived so late that, for many Ethiopians, the new rains had already ended the crisis. Much of the food arrived, ironically, "as local farmers were bringing in their first good harvests in years." Harvests that, unfortunately, were now worthless to those impoverished farmers because the country was flooded with free grain. There wasn't even warehouse space to store the local harvest. And the free grain kept pouring in, nonetheless.

To people living through it, it must have seemed like an episode of *The Twilight Zone*.

They had survived a three- to four-year drought with little, if any, outside aid and assistance. They had watched friends and family wither and die. Now it was finally over. The rains had come, the crops were good. Finally, there was food to eat and money to be made. And then suddenly there were these massive shipments of outside grain showing up everywhere. The farmer's hard-won harvests were suddenly worthless.

And those impoverished farmers were the lucky ones. Because to have a harvest at all (even a worthless one) meant that they had done the almost impossible—that they had held onto their land through the bad times. That they had kept enough of their possessions to be able to buy seed for that long-awaited good season.

For the others—the vast majority—it was worse. They had no harvests to compete with the free foreign grain because they had long since lost their land to famine. For them, the food simply arrived too late. As Timberlake points out, the relief shipments that were finally delivered were "handed out only after people had been driven off their own land and assembled in famine camps. Had [relief] arrived earlier, farmers could have stayed on their land and rehabilitated it so they would have been ready for the return of the rains."

But, you might think, surely such food will help *someone* when it finally does arrive. Perhaps the ones whose images spurred people and agencies to action are long gone, but (and you are, unfortunately, right) others will certainly have come to take their place. Surely *some* of this food can reach *some* of these people early enough in their hunger to save them.

In fact, as many of you may have already heard from other sources, much of the food in famine relief shipments never gets to anyone. Even in the best circumstances—no war, no serious logistical problems—only about 75 percent of the food that reaches a nation in need is ever distributed. In the Sudan relief effort, explains Timberlake, it was 64 percent. And in circumstances that are less than ideal, the situation is much worse.

I sit here, surrounded by books, scientific articles, government reports, Rodale Institute studies, newspaper clippings, scholarly writings—all with the same, sad message: The food just doesn't get there.

On a bright, sunny Saturday near the close of February 1990, I can't take my eyes—and my mind—off one such clipping. The newspaper article is less than a week old, but could have been written, with little change, a decade ago:

Washington, DC
Associated Press
The lives of up to five million Ethiopians are at risk because antigovernment forces have shut down a port that has been the key entry point for outside food assistance, U.S. officials say.

To the West, U.S. officials say a crisis is rapidly developing in Sudan, where a bitter civil war has prevented the transport of relief supplies to rebel-held territory in the southern part of the country.

Renewed fighting has led to the suspension of food flights to southern Sudan, and the government also is preventing the departure of a relief train along a route where food shortages are severe. The rebels also have been blocking relief efforts.

Estimates of the number of Sudanese people affected by famine range between one million and three million.

Responding to international protests set off by the offensive and the damage to relief operations, the Eritrean's People's Liberation Front said it had initiated the fighting to preempt the Ethiopian government from using the food aid as a weapon in the war.

The Eritrean front apparently fears that the government would only give the food to its supporters or use it to coerce support.

The impending famine evokes memories of the 1984–85 period in Ethiopia, when more than a million people died.

The article concludes with the fact that "more than $70 million" of U.S. money is involved. Seventy million dollars worth of food that will probably never reach the people for whom it is intended.

I have all too many such articles sitting on my desk. The situation is not uncommon. Famine today is rarely caused by drought or crop failure alone. There is almost always war involved as well. Unfortunately, food shipments often *fuel* those wars. As the articles make clear, the food itself is a reason to fight—something to fight over. The rebels are halting the shipments because they say they should be the ones to distribute it, to choose who gets fed and who does not.

The government is doing the same because of fears that the rebels will get the food. They fear the rebels will use the food to gain civilian support. They fear the food will directly sustain the soldiers who fight for the rebel cause. And they fear that the rebels will sell the food to buy more guns and weapons.

That's the part of this section you most likely don't want to hear: That relief shipments often fuel these cruel foreign wars in a very direct manner. All too often, food meant to relieve the effects of famine instead feeds soldiers on both sides who are by all accounts as much of a threat to the people as any shortage of food.

You send money to feed starving people and the food it buys is stolen. The food is eaten by soldiers, fueling their acts of cruelty. The food is sold on the black market to buy guns and ammunition.

Sorry. But, like we said before, you have to face the reality of the situation before you can hope to change it. If it helps, be assured that I dislike this reality as much as you do.

But I accept that it is reality. And this reality is yet another reason that I choose to think small in the solutions I propose in the second half of this book. No massive shipments of valuable food and equipment that can be hijacked and turned into cash and death. No plantations that destroy the land, feed the deserts, and are themselves open to raids and pillaging.

Small solutions. Too small for powerful people to trifle with. Too small for an army or a group of soldiers to care about. Too small to attract a lot of attention in troubled times. But big enough to feed the family who tends this small solution.

I'm sure you're as anxious as I am to get on with it, to define those small solutions so that we can all begin working on them. But just one more thing must be addressed here in the "problems" sections of this book, and that's the financial aspect of famine relief. I don't mean the money we send to feed the victims of famine. I mean the money the victims have spent before they reach those camps, before our cameras take their pictures.

We've talked about how many of these people are simply too far gone medically for our food to help them return to a normal life. Unfortunately, their financial situation deteriorates in the same way. And, in a particularly vicious cycle, their poverty lays the groundwork for future famines.

Almost all experts agree that poverty breeds famine. It's not hard to understand how. After all, some people in developing countries do have money. Or if they don't have money, they have things they can sell or trade—what the experts call *assets*. And people with money or assets—even in the middle of the most miserable famine imaginable—can always find food to buy.

That may surprise you, but famine really doesn't mean that there isn't food around. In fact, there is almost always food *for sale* in famine-affected areas. But those who abandon their farms and march to the camps simply have nothing left with which to buy that food.

As the authors of *Preventing Famine* point out,

> Major droughts are times of great "shaking out" in [rural society]. Livestock, jewelry, even land are sold at ruinous prices in the desperation to survive.
>
> To be saved by famine relief is to come away with virtually nothing but your life.

That's a pretty strong statement, but unfortunately right on the mark. The authors also note the endless cycle of famine, poverty, and famine, and agree that prevention is the only true solution. Relief, they explain, simply breeds poverty. And poverty, of course, makes a person extremely vulnerable to famine:

> Failure to prevent famine, but only to relieve it after it is substantially advanced, is probably the single greatest cause of increased [poverty] among rural people in drought-prone environments.
>
> Long-term measures for famine prevention are therefore those which increase and protect the assets of the poor.

Exactly. *Prevention,* not relief. There, I've said it! I had vowed that I wouldn't speak directly against relief because I didn't want to offend anyone. But my typing fingers simply refuse to obey my cautious mind. They yield to my growing awareness that relief is more than just not an answer to famine. It is a *cause* of famine.

The rich get richer, the poor get hungrier. As famine expert Lloyd Timberlake says, "Moving free or cheap food from country to country is a very inefficient way of seeing to it that the hungry eat." You cannot examine the reality of relief programs as they exist today and not come away agreeing with him. The only difference is that your own words might be much stronger.

As Timberlake explains, the massive shipments of food that are the centerpoint of famine relief programs involve a great deal of money changing hands. Sadly, those of us who have studied famine realize all too well that these shipments are often motivated as much by profit as by charity.

Yes, hungry people are getting some food, but often it's food that other people want to sell, not what the recipients want—or need— to eat. One of the less well known negative aspects of relief programs is that those huge shipments provide windfall profits to nations anxious to get rid of unwanted surpluses of food. Food that's often inappropriate for consumption by the poor, hungry people it may eventually reach.

As Timberlake explains in *The Politics of Food Aid,* "Nations with food surpluses tend to be more interested in getting rid of that food in ways that benefit the producing nations rather than the recipient countries." Even the normally conservative World Bank is quoted as agreeing that "food aid is more closely related to the needs of donors than those of recipients."

The end result can be worse than just ugly economics. As in our Mexican example, this kind of development has the potential to do much harm. And, again, as in the case we earlier cited in Mexico, things often don't get better for the people involved until funding for the program helping them is discontinued. To illustrate the point, Timberlake refers to a study of a mother-and-child nutrition program in Central America:

> Children's nutrition improved only when the programme ceased. When the [program-provided] grain and butter fat was available, mothers fed their children only that. They had, after all, been told how good this foreign food was for their children.
>
> When it was not available, they returned to giving their children traditional fare, local fruits and vegetables, which contained a lot of vitamins and minerals not found in the "supplementary" food.

Economic problems are also involved. Many critics have accused the United States and Europe of using relief programs to solve their own crisis of domestic overproduction. After all, it's well known that the United States and Europe grow too much grain and produce too much butter. So, to keep farmers from being destroyed by the inevitable result (low prices) of their own overproduction, those food products are subsidized. What a farmer can't sell, the government buys.

And, of course, those huge stockpiles provide a powerful incentive to continue justifying massive shipments of food to other nations. The system (shipping food vast distances to starving people) may not work, the food may not get to the right people (it almost certainly can't get there in time when a specific emergency threatens), and it may well be the wrong food for those people. But the prevailing attitude is "Hey, we had too much corn or butter and we got rid of it. We got a good price for it and we got to say that we contributed to solving the hunger problem. So the system works, and everybody benefits!"

The truth is that much of the food—even that which does reach the right people—is not eaten because it is just not the right food to send. All too often, especially in shipments that ease the massive grain surpluses of U.S. farmers, it's *yellow* corn that's sent to places like Africa. But, as we said earlier, *white* corn is eaten there almost exclusively. Yellow corn is really more suited to animal feed than to any other purpose. And, of course, almost all that corn is grown using chemical farming methods. The land on which it's grown here in America is slowly stripped of fertility while the water supplies are polluted for miles around.

That's a poor system for everyone except those making short-term profits from it. As many people have pointed out, if simply getting corn to hungry people were the point, the donors could buy that corn a lot closer to the people and save a fortune on shipping costs. But the point is really to get rid of our own surplus under the guise of charity.

Australia showed us how to do it the right way, Timberlake says. In 1985–86, the Australians sent twenty-three tons of corn to Mozambique, Ethiopia, and Somalia. But they didn't ship Australian surplus. Instead, they bought corn in nearby Zimbabwe, which had enough of a surplus to sell—but not give—to their hungry neighbors.

And it was the right kind of corn—white corn, the kind of corn these people love to eat. The corn they are used to eating—that they know how to prepare. The corn that is now a part of their culture.

And what do we do? During the same period of time, the United States shipped twenty-eight tons of U.S. corn to Mozambique. Yellow corn, of course. Grown for animal feed.

Who did the most good? The country that supported the agriculture of a developing African nation and delivered a lot of culturally acceptable food to starving people—while spending almost all the money on food itself and little on transportation (which no one, after all, can eat)—or the nation that saw a chance to get rid of tons of unwanted surplus even if it meant depressing the prices that other Africans could get for their locally grown crops?

I know many of you are angry right now. It's hard not to be. But I believe this to be an accurate representation of the facts.

And I can tell you from my travels worldwide that people in many other nations are angry at the United States (and some European nations as well) for not solving our overproduction problems in another way, one that doesn't threaten starving people.

Would it really be so bad for U.S. farmers to stop chemically growing all this extra, unnecessary, unwanted corn? Would it be so bad to change tactics, look for other solutions to our farming problems, and actually help the starving people of the Third World—without a catch?

So far, not many Americans are urging those in charge to look at what's really happening. So far, there is very little public pressure to make us accountable for the true, long-term costs of the way we dole out foreign aid. And there is even less public awareness that these massive shipments of food that flood poor nations greatly depress the prices that local farmers can get for their own food—the food that *they've* grown. According to this largely overlooked economic argument against relief shipments, not only is the food that enters the country of dubious value, but it also serves to keep poor farmers poor by making their own hard-earned harvest worthless as well.

Originally, we planned to title this book *Famine Prevention: The 90 Percent Solution*. There are several reasons why we picked those words. One was simply that I didn't wish to understate the magnitude of the problem. I didn't want to imply that we were going to be 100 percent successful. If we could make things nine-tenths better, that would save millions of lives. Besides, my editor and I felt that the "90 Percent" in the title would catch people's eyes and attention. "Why 90 percent? Why not 100 percent?" we hoped they would ask—and be intrigued enough to buy the book and find out the answer.

The other reason was that the 90 percent figure kept showing up in many different places. One example, to which we devote an entire chapter later on, is that women do 90 percent of the work growing food in many parts of the Third World. So any solutions to the famine problem must be solutions that recognize that fact and make women's lives easier.

We encountered that figure again when we learned that 90 percent of the crops grown in Africa today are not native to the area. They are imported crops, and growing them often requires huge amounts of fertilizers and pesticides to keep them alive in their alien environment. We feel this kind of "backward agriculture" increases vulnerability to insect and disease devastation and practically invites famine.

Yet another 90 percent figure is the one I wish to discuss here. And that is the estimate—from the Hunger Project and others— that 90 percent of all people who die from hunger do so *outside* of famines. That's right. Only 10 percent of the people in the world who die from not having enough to eat are actually victims of famines. The vast majority—the other 90 percent—die of chronic, persistent hunger. Somehow, although writing a book ostensibly about preventing famines, I knew I had to include those people in our solutions. And so their plight guided our thoughts all the way. They *are* the "90 percent solution," because if our work didn't include them, then we really wouldn't be doing a very good job of attacking the reality of world hunger.

I believe the solutions we propose in the following chapters protect those people as well as the victims of outright famines. And that is why I still think sometimes of this book as "the 90 percent solution"—because the solutions we propose are just as effective at reducing that hunger—the hunger that slowly, almost imperceptibly decimates health and lives—as they are at preventing deadly famines. Organizations that attack this hidden tragedy (such as the Hunger Project, which has produced an excellent short video on the subject, entitled "Famine and Chronic Persistent Hunger—A Life and Death Distinction") fight a truly courageous, uphill-all-the-way battle. Theirs is the most difficult job of all. (The nonprofit Hunger Project has 5.8 million members, from 152 countries—a truly international group.)

The technical definition of a famine requires that people be on the move, that they leave the area in which they live and engage in a grueling death march. Sometimes that march is to another area that they pray is fertile enough to support them. But most often they march toward a rumor of assistance-provided food. Toward the hope of a relief camp.

Sometimes those camps are there. Often they are not. Sometimes they are there, but terribly short of food. The loss of life in those camps is often felt to be greater than if the people had remained in their local villages. But rumors and hopes can be powerful, so the people march.

They are, by definition, the victims of famine: the 10 percent who get all the publicity because they have fulfilled that definition—simply by not staying put. By marching, they *become* a famine. And, by being so declared, by meeting the official criteria and being so visible, they become news.

The march forces a situation of not-enough-food to be called a famine. And then, however slowly and however inappropriately, the world mobilizes to send some sort of food to that region. But the other 90 percent of the world's people dying from the situation of not-enough-food are totally invisible. They stay put. They do not march. They are not part of a famine. And so in many ways they simply do not count.

In truth, those people *are* difficult to see. The distinction between a dangerously hungry village and one that is just typically poor is often minuscule and easily blurred. We are talking about hunger that can come so close to bare-bones adequate nutrition that it may take years to claim its victims.

Yes, we are talking about victims who die of classic malnutrition. But more frequently, the actual cause of death is influenza, dysentery, measles, the common cold. More children who fall victim to this hidden hunger die of diarrhea than any other single cause. Hunger in this form is a kind of non-infectious AIDS, because it simply weakens its victim's immune system to the point where almost any minor medical problem becomes a fatal disease.

Remember, we are talking about people who may have some food to eat—just never quite enough. Such people may consistently get 85 percent of their minimum requirement of protein, 92 percent of the minimum of some vitamins, 80 percent of the minerals needed to thrive. When this situation is repeated year after year, those seemingly minor deficiencies exact a terrible toll—but not so terrible that it's obvious. Not so terrible that the victims sell off their possessions and march for help. After all, there is always some food to eat. It is a silent crisis, a sinister threat.

In fact, the process is so slow that the result has become something considered the norm. A mother passes away at forty-five, a father at thirty-six, leaving behind three children out of the eight who were born.

If these people understood their plight—if they could see their future and recognize the alternatives that existed—perhaps they would march and so be declared in need of an outpouring of assistance. Then at least they would share in the supplemental food that eventually flows to famines. But because they do not march, they do not count. There are no massive fund-raising efforts in their behalf. And yet nine of them perish for every one person claimed by famine.

The solutions that we propose to prevent famine will, by their very nature, attack this hidden hunger as well. By building up the capacity of local peoples to grow larger amounts of more nutritious food on marginal land, our solutions will ease the "food debt" that causes chronic, persistent hunger on an almost daily basis.

The tragedy, in a sense, is that so little help is needed. Just increasing by very small percentages the amounts of food that these people can raise would be all that is necessary to cheat hunger of its victims. Luckily, there is no way to implement our famine prevention solutions without attacking the invisible tragedy of chronic, persistent hunger along the way.

But those who concentrate only on famines, those whose efforts at relief recognize only the people who march to the camps, are letting hunger off the hook. They are allowing themselves to be deceived by the spectacle of the famine march. They see only the surface of the iceberg and not the massive chunk of suffering and death that floats below.

Famines get the press. They get donations. They get public awareness. And by doing so they effectively doom the vast majority of hunger's victims. Victims who are not nearly so far gone, and yet are in just as much danger. Victims who need just a little help to be saved.

But make no mistake. Without that help, they *will* die. Currently, 35,000 people a day die from hunger—mostly children. On average, 31,500 of them die from chronic, persistent hunger, not famines.

You could give a million dollars a day in donations to famine relief and still not save them.

Enough problems—it's time for solutions. I hope you're still with me. I must admit that sometimes even I get a bit down when I dwell on the failures of famine relief. The problems and the complications involved can seem overwhelming—too much to bear, too big to beat. But they're not. I believe that we as a nation can face up to the situation and change things for the better. We must. There is simply no other alternative.

Too many hungry people are depending on us. We *must* begin to spin the globe in another direction, to turn relief that doesn't work into something that does.

The point has been made that we have interfered in these people's lives and made them vulnerable to famine. The point has been made that development in the traditional sense has only made these people more vulnerable. And I certainly trust that we have made the very sad point that famine relief doesn't work, that it often hurts. That it serves to keep poor people poor. And that it misses the vast majority of hungry people who need help.

I hope that those points are now clear because I have hundreds more examples of the problems associated with relief—examples I desperately *don't* want to drag out. It's much too easy to get trapped wallowing in the depth of these problems. I want to move on. I want to leave the dark past behind and look toward the bright future that I truly believe is waiting to be fulfilled.

I know it's there. I see glimpses of it in my travels. I see many organizations out there—including our own nonprofit arm, the Rodale Institute/Rodale International—already helping to make that future a reality by doing good work, the right way.

That bright future is already beginning. With *small* successes in *small* areas. Make no mistake. I want to keep things small. But I also want to greatly increase the number of small successes out there.

We know that relief doesn't work; we know that development doesn't work. So let's try something that does. Not aid. Not relief. Not development.

Let's try prevention, famine prevention. A plan to reverse the vulnerability that colonialism and wrong-headed development attempts have caused. A plan that makes use of native resources, of methods that have proven themselves over centuries. A long-term solution that restores the basic rights and cultures of developing people, that eases their personal debt (and, quite likely, their national debt as well), that puts food on the table and wood on the fire, and helps women to attain a greater status in their society.

A plan that reduces the vulnerability of people around the world—including us—to famine's effects.

To end Part One, a vision of what *hasn't* worked: A rusting tractor sitting in the shifting sands of a growing desert. An empty chemical drum nearby. No people. No sounds. No life. To begin Part Two, a vision of a new Africa: That same land, green and lush. Lanes of tall trees with a variety of crops growing in between. Children are playing with goats. The women can read. They no longer carry a look of perpetual exhaustion. People laugh by the fire. As always, a traveler is welcomed quickly.

You can be the force that shifts these visions. You can choose which image will actually greet people's eyes ten or twenty years from now. You can help lessen the vulnerability of millions of people—and protect yourself and your descendants from famine's effects as well.

Enough of the past. It's time to look forward. Time to "save three lives." Come with me now as—together—we examine the plan for famine prevention.

Part Two

The Rodale Plan
for Famine
Prevention

CHAPTER FIVE

Foods That
Defy Drought

A few chapters back, we discussed the damage that plantation farming has caused in Africa. We talked about how this method of planting massive stands of single, and often overbred, species has drained the soil of nutrients and encouraged the spread of weeds and insects. But there is another side effect of the plantation farming method that we only briefly alluded to.

Remember, all the way back in the first chapter, when we mentioned the people whose lives had supposedly been improved, but who were complaining about the loss of their native plants, plants that had been grown in their culture for untold centuries?

Many of those plants, of course, were uprooted to make room for the corn, cotton, coffee, and cassava farms. Even in the smaller home gardens, cash crops were encouraged by the developers—the "experts"—at the expense of native plants.

In fact, the traditional practice of growing a wide variety of those old native plants was actively discouraged. The experts said they were a waste of space and there was no market for them. Yet those plants are the single most important component of any plan to prevent famine. That's because they *are* "famine plants."

That name has two, very distinct meanings. "Famine plants" are nutritious, tough survivors that can help the humans who recognize the potential of these plants to weather the fiercest famine. When all the fragile imported crops have been killed off by drought or the heavy seasonal rains, these plants are still around.

There's no magic involved. These plants can resist harsh times better simply because they're native to the area—they've weathered the natural cycle of droughts and excessive rainfall for centuries.

Famine plants have very low water requirements, yet many can also tolerate huge amounts of rainfall in a short period of time. Corn and other imported plants need massive amounts of water to thrive. They suffer greatly in times of drought, and don't do well during harsh, heavy rains, either.

But that's because those plantation plants are not native to Africa. Famine plants are. Extended droughts and heavy rains are not news to them. They're used to adversity. And they provide a very nutritious meal. Sometimes medicine as well.

To the experts, these local species are also known as famine plants. And they are observed very carefully—but for what I consider to be a perverse reason. The famine experts do not consider such plants to be useful food. To these experts—the intellectuals, the academic studiers of famine—they are only considered useful as indicators of oncoming disaster. They note that, most of the time, these plants grow wild and are not eaten. And when the people start to eat the famine plants, the experts say, "Uh-oh—I think things are starting to get bad." And they call up Chicago or Birmingham or wherever and say, "Gear up and get the trucks rolling because we're going to need relief."

To the experts, famine plants are an *indication* that a problem is arising. To my eyes, they are the *solution* to that same problem.

I must give credit for much of my thinking on famine plants to Dr. John Robson, an English physician. Back in the late 1950s and early 1960s, Dr. Robson did famine relief work in Tanganyika, which later merged with Zanzibar to become the country of Tanzania. Although a pretty serious famine was underway, he noted that the people in the cities were suffering much more than the people in the countryside. When he went out into the countryside to investigate, he saw that the land was very dry, but the people didn't look nearly as bad as you would expect under the circumstances. Actually, they were doing O.K.

So he asked them, "What are you eating?"

And they said, "Well, the corn crop failed and we don't have any rice, but we are eating these plants over here in the bush."

He thought they were weeds. But he looked closer and saw that the plants they were pointing to were green and growing despite the drought. And the people were eating the seeds and leaves of those plants.

To Dr. Robson, this was unusual. But, in truth, it's really representative of the way Africans have fed themselves for centuries. As my good friend Bede Okigbo has explained to me, 90 percent of the food grown in Africa that is eaten by Africans comes from home gardens. Actually, only we would call them home gardens; Africans call them farms.

These farm-gardens are small areas—generally around two to five acres. Some corn, some native plants, and some other things are usually included. They look, to the casual observer, like scraggly patches of random plants and trees.

But they are not. As Okigbo has explained to me, they are actually very highly organized plots. And they almost always include the kind of plants that the people who were surviving the famine showed to Dr. Robson—what both he and Okigbo call "semidomesticated" plants.

Such plants aren't weeds, but they aren't really crops either. They are plants that the Africans have been relying on for thousands of years for food in difficult times. They probably had been weeds at

one time, weeds that the people had improved somewhat by select-
ing better strains—often simply by pulling up the weedier varieties. But because they weren't regularly relied on, they were never
fully bred, like the fruits and vegetables we are accustomed to.
(Everything we eat today, after all, started out as a wild plant and
was deliberately bred to the form it now has.) And that's exactly
what Dr. Robson says that we should do with famine plants. Breed
them. Select the better ones, work with them a bit, make them even
better, and then give back to the African farmers a range of improved versions of their own neglected native plants.

Since these plants are native to the area, they already have natural, ingrown abilities to resist pests and disease. Obviously, you
want to select the ones that do so best. You also want to be careful to
breed enough variety that farmers can have several—all very natural, not overly bred—strains growing in any one area.

Famine plants are obviously very resistant to drought. And we
know that they thrive with little or no attention, because they survive with no human cultivation or intervention between droughts
and floods. These plants are eaten heartily by the people in bad
times and, many years ago, had a place in every garden even during
good times. They are so hardy, however, that even when they were
formally banished from many home gardens by expert decree, they
survived nearby without human cultivation. They hung on—
viewed as weeds by those who knew no better—on the garden's
edge. Often they had to hold their place against weeds in the brush,
or in scrub areas far away from the cultivated plots.

Nutritious multipurpose crops. Tough as weeds. What a combination! Really, all you have to do with these famine plants is *not*
deliberately pull them all up and they'll be there when you need
them.

And they're more nutritious than foreign foods. Dr. Robson is a
nutritionist as well as a physician. He analyzed some of those native
plants (we'll discuss some in detail later) and found out two impor-

tant things. One was that you couldn't get as many bushels per acre of edible food from them as you could from foreign crops like corn. But he also discovered that the bushels you *did* get were much more nutritious than the cultivated crops. One famine plant in particular provided more protein than corn! Acre for acre, he found that famine plants could provide more nutrition than the plantation crops. And, of course, they would continue to do so during times of famine and drought.

So he went to the FAO—the Food and Agriculture Organization of the United Nations—where he is now an advisory board member, and he said, "Look, we've been doing this all wrong. We have to turn around the way we do things, by taking the famine plants and making them into full-fledged crops."

They laughed at him. They said, "That's going backward. We don't want to go backward; we want to go forward—by planting more improved strains of corn and wheat. The solution to this hunger problem is to start up fertilizer factories and get tractors over here. We'll grow so much corn your famine plants won't mean anything."

So he got absolutely nowhere.

Years went by. As we know all too well, the corn and other cash crops were planted in massive amounts—slowly destroying the African soil as well as the way of life of its people. Vulnerability to famine increased dramatically. Dr. Robson left Africa and took a teaching position at the University of Michigan. And that's when another piece of the puzzle fell into place.

There is an archeological dig at a place in southern Illinois called the Koster site. They discovered it fifteen or twenty years ago, and as they excavated layer after layer, they realized that people had been living at the base of the cliffs along the Illinois River. Every time they'd clean out a layer, they'd find the remains of an even earlier village underneath. They had dug pretty deep and found food remains, including seeds. So they called the university. And Dr. Robson was part of the nutritional archeology team sent out to the dig.

He looked at the seeds and could see right away that they were amaranth seeds. He got out of the pit, looked around, and saw that amaranth was growing wild all along the river. Amaranth was one of the most widely eaten of the famine plants that he had seen when he was in Africa.

What an astonishing discovery! Plants that had obviously been vital to the food supply of the early native Americans were still being used by native people in Africa to offset the effects of famine!

Using the better equipment available at the university, he repeated his nutritional analysis. Now he could check the amino acid content of the plants as well as their protein content. Not only did the analysis confirm that amaranth is higher in protein than corn, but Robson also found that the plant is rich in the essential amino acid lysine. Corn is deficient in lysine. Even half-wild, this weed-food-crop that now seemed to be native to almost everywhere was clearly nutritionally superior to corn.

But people still weren't listening. The university wouldn't give Dr. Robson any research money to study amaranth further.

So he wrote a letter to me in June 1973. It has been my experience that every ten years or so I get what I call a real letter—a super, first-class letter that changes my life when I open it. This letter from Dr. Robson was one of those. It wasn't a long letter. He briefly told me the story about famine plants and the Koster site discovery, explaining how the university and the food industry wouldn't give him any money and that he had written to us as his last hope.

And I immediately thought, "This is one of those ten-year letters! I'm not going to simply answer it. I'm going to go there." The next day I was in Ann Arbor asking him, "What do we do next?" He said he needed $10,000 and that the first step would be to send a student to Mexico to get samples of the native amaranth that grows there.

Amaranth, it turns out, has a long and very interesting history in the Western Hemisphere. It was one of the main staples of the early, highly advanced civilizations like the Mayas, the Incas, and the Aztecs. But because it was also an essential element in those people's cultures (including their sacrificial rites), Cortez and his soldiers did their best to eliminate its cultivation and use when they invaded.

Nobody knows if amaranth actually originated in Central America or in Africa. It probably is common to both, since back in the early stages of our planet's development, those two continents were joined. Slightly different strains of amaranth probably developed in each area after the continents split apart millions of years ago.

I know I'm getting a little bit off the track here, but I beg your indulgence for just a bit longer. You see, amaranth is very exciting to me. Since those early days, we've ("we" being the nonprofit Rodale Institute) invested millions of dollars in gathering amaranth from around the world, carefully studying it, and growing large fields of many varieties at the Rodale Research Center's Experimental Farms. So, with at least this one famine plant, we are pretty much ready. Ready to give a variety of improved, but still very natural, strains of this wonderful ancient food crop back to the people who originally semidomesticated it.

But it wasn't all that long ago that U.S. Customs almost prevented this integral aspect of our famine prevention plan from ever beginning.

Just this one brief story, and then we'll get back to the famine prevention plan: Obviously, we had to begin by collecting lots of amaranth seeds—especially the white seed type, which is more of a "crop" than the black seed variety, which is mostly a "weed." So we gave Dr. Robson the money and he sent a student by the name of Joel Elias to Mexico to collect varieties of the white seed and bring it back. We never even considered what was going to happen when he tried to re-enter the United States with a 50-pound bag of seeds! Of course, the customs agents stopped him. They explained that he had to have a permit from the U.S. Department of Agriculture (USDA) to bring in that much seed, and that this bag's contents would have to be destroyed.

Elias started talking to the agent in charge, explaining that the seed was necessary for a research project, that it was very important, and that a lot of money had been invested. "I'm not just some kook," he said. "I'm from the University of Michigan."

The agent asked, "Is that who you're doing this for? Who's behind it?"

"Actually," he replied, "I'm doing it for Bob Rodale. For *Organic Gardening* magazine."

So the agent said, "Bob Rodale? Why didn't you say so? *I* get *Organic Gardening*! Go right ahead. You can take it through."

That's a true story. And what makes it even stranger is that the next year we needed more seed. We sent the same student, and he got the same agent at the border!

Anyway, back to that first year. I got the letter in June, and we had to plant by the Fourth of July to get a crop in that year. Thanks to our customs official subscriber, we got the seed in by July 1. In September we had amaranth growing all over the place. Many different varieties—big ones, little ones.

Besides having edible leaves and providing an extremely nutritious grain from its huge seed heads, amaranth is a spectacularly beautiful plant—extraordinarily colorful. I call it a movie star of a plant. It is simply the most beautiful crop plant possible. And wherever it grows in the world, it is also involved in the mysticism and the religion of the people, as well. (That's why Cortez and those who followed him worked so hard to eradicate it. Even in Mexico today, it is still considered to be a sign of rebellion against those ancient conquerors to eat a very popular local food—a kind of caramel popcorn cake—made with popped amaranth.) Amaranth is not just a thing to eat, it is a thing of the spirit.

We began improving the plants—basically trying to find the varieties that were the most drought resistant, had the biggest seed heads, and were of fairly uniform height to make harvesting easier. But we also wanted to be sure that amaranth could really be grown everywhere.

So I wrote an article about it in *Organic Gardening* and asked for volunteers from every state to try to grow it. I said, "Write to us and we'll send you some seed." Over a thousand people responded and we finally sent seed out to three or four hundred of them.

It was a perfect year for this experiment because it was very dry—and our only rule was that you couldn't water the amaranth. We found that it needed a little bit of moisture to sprout, but after that it would set seed everywhere—even in the driest areas. The test was a tremendous success, and we got the kind of data in one year that would have taken a decade by conventional methods.

And we later found out that some of those readers were university scientists who kept at it. Years later, we'd get letters saying, "I've been working with this amaranth for five years now. Would you like to know what I've found?" The end result is that we know a tremendous amount about amaranth's potential to provide a double source of nutritious food—greens and grain—in very harsh climates. And all because Dr. Robson had such very strong feelings about the need to *respect* the people of the Third World.

"Our role is not to force them to do things, to change the way they live," he told me once. "Our role is to help them do better with what they have."

Other experts just looked at the natives eating the famine plants and called them "weed eaters." Even our farm manager at the time—the person whose job it was to plant research crops for us— said "No!" That's a weed! You can't pay me enough to plant weeds!" He finally agreed, but it showed me just how strong this prejudice against noncorn, noncash crops really was—we even had it at our own Research Center! So you can imagine what the people at the major agricultural universities must have thought.

As best I can figure, the Rodale Institute has put about $5 million into amaranth research and improvement. And famine prevention was always the basic motivation.

You have to realize that, had this plant not been virtually out-lawed for centuries by the Spaniards, grain-producing amaranth might today be as common a crop as corn or beans. It certainly was before Columbus came here. (Just imagine how beautiful the Mid-west would look covered with these tall, leafy red, gold, orange, and purple plants instead of corn!)

And what we're proposing—substituting these improved strains of native plants for the foreign, poorly chosen current crops of Africa—is really not all that outlandish. A century ago, soy-beans, sunflowers, and peanuts were considered unworthy of re-search. These crops, like amaranth today, weren't taken seriously. Their supporters fought a long, hard battle, uphill all the way. Now they are staples for much of the world.

Here are a few facts about amaranth. The plant's broad leaves are mild flavored (they're delicious in a salad), and rich in protein, vi-tamins, and minerals. In much of the world, the leaves and stems of young plants are also boiled as greens. In Greece, the leaves have been boiled and eaten in salads since the days of the *Iliad* and the

Odyssey. In North American deserts, where the scorching sun bolts lettuce and blanches cabbage, amaranth has long been a major source of nutritious greens for local Indians.

A U.S. Department of Agriculture bulletin (Martin and Telek, 1979) once noted that starting from seed, amaranth can produce delectable spinachlike greens in five weeks or less, can continue to produce a crop of edible leaves weekly for up to six months, and will then yield thousands of seeds. And amaranth is a mighty producer of cereal-like grain. A single plant can easily produce 50,000 of those small, edible seeds.

The average protein content of amaranth seeds is 16 percent. Wheat averages 14 percent protein, rice 8 percent, corn 12 percent. The protein in amaranth, unlike that in those better-known grains, is considered to be nutritionally balanced. The protein in those other grains lacks enough of the essential amino acid lysine to provide optimum nourishment for humans. But amaranth's lysine content (three times that of corn) is equal to that found in milk—the standard of nutritional excellence the world over. Amaranth grain comes closer than any other grain protein to the perfect balance of amino acids required in the human diet, and the lysine is of special benefit to infants, children, and pregnant and lactating women.

When amaranth grains are heated, they pop to produce a nutty-flavored "popcorn." Mixed with honey, popped amaranth becomes the treat that Mexicans still eat with relish today, to enjoy the flavor, to thumb their noses at their ancient conquerors, and to once again spiritually commune with their ancestors who, fueled by amaranth, built those legendary civilizations so long ago. A similar preparation, known as *laddoos,* is popular in northern India. A strain of amaranth there is known is *ramdana,* meaning "seed sent by God."

The USDA bulletin says that "For little effort [amaranth] affords a nutritious dish with abundant provitamin A, a vitamin particularly necessary in the tropics for eye health." Millions of dollars are now spent on projects that give vitamin A supplements to children in Africa and other tropical areas in order to prevent the blindness that still afflicts thousands of children every year. Eating locally grown amaranth could eliminate the vitamin A deficiency that causes this horror and would make those supplements largely unnecessary. And amaranth leaves are also an excellent source of vitamin C, niacin, and potassium.

For Third World peoples and U.S. farmers alike, amaranth has much potential as a cash crop. The starch that makes up the bulk of processed amaranth flour has a unique structure. Researchers say it is likely to prove useful for applications in the food, plastics, cosmetics, and other industries. Amaranth also has important potential as a base for natural dyes (remember—it is the single most colorful plant you're ever likely to see) and in the pharmaceutical industry. And 20 percent of the seed is an edible oil whose possibilities have yet to be fully explored, although it's already known that 70 percent of the oil is composed of the highly desirable oleic and linoleic acids. With this wide array of spinoffs—nutritious greens, cereal-like grain seeds, vegetable oil, industrial applications, and extraction of vitamins for natural supplement manufacture—amaranth could well become the ultimate cash crop.

For the natives themselves, amaranth foods can be prepared easily with simple, low-energy techniques. Cleaned, unprocessed whole grain can be made into a highly nutritious porridge by simply boiling it briefly in water. Toasted or popped, the grain becomes a very tasty food that requires no further preparation. You can even sprout the grain and eat the sprouts!

A pound of amaranth greens provides two to three times the amount of nutrients found in a pound of other vegetables. Compared to other potherbs, amaranth is exceptionally high in calcium and iron. And yields of almost twenty tons of greens per acre per year have been reported. And, of course, amaranth is exceptionally hardy, grows in the driest of climates, and requires virtually no cultivation.

Amaranth is what got me interested in famine prevention. It seemed that wherever I went—Africa, Mexico, Illinois—amaranth had a long history. Obviously, we could do much to help make the African people less vulnerable to famine's effects by helping them re-establish this significant famine plant.

And, thanks to the hard work of my associates at our experimental farms, we now have over a thousand varieties to offer. Rodale International, a branch of the Rodale Institute that's very active in Africa, has already helped farmers plant amaranth in many parts of the globe. But amaranth is just one local plant that deserves attention. We know of dozens more that also have tremendous potential. And hundreds more are just waiting to be studied.

The National Academy of Sciences (NAS) and its operations arm, the National Research Council (NRC), have done some great work in areas that are essential to any realistic plan for famine prevention. Recently, NAS and NRC issued a report—entitled *Underexploited Indigenous Crops of Africa*—on the kinds of plants we're talking about. The report referred to them as " 'life-support plants' that the poor rely on to keep themselves alive in times of drought or other hardship." The report concludes that very little is known about most of these crops and that some are so neglected they are in serious danger of extinction. In some sense, they report, all we know is that we don't know enough about them. The native people who *do* know are rapidly losing that knowledge. But one thing is certain—the plants themselves are desperately needed by hungry people.

From the NAS-NRC booklet, here is a partial listing, most of which comes from my good friend Noel Vietmeyer, perhaps the person in the world with the most knowledge about these potential superstar famine prevention plants (Vietmeyer is now a senior program officer for the NAS Board on Science and Technology for International Development):

• *The African Yam Bean.* This root crop produces high-protein tubers (like potatoes), a nutritious seed, *and* edible leaves. "It can be grown in infertile, weathered soils (and) where rainfall is extremely heavy. Although highly regarded among the people of tropical Africa, the crop is virtually unknown to science."

• *The Bambara Groundnut.* This is a legume (a plant that literally "pulls" the essential plant-growing element nitrogen from the air, thus providing free fertilizer for other nearby crops) that grows underground, like a peanut. The NAS-NRC booklet describes it as "a rare example in which nature provides a complete food." It thrives in dry, inferior soils where peanuts fail, it resists pests and disease and, if managed well, gives high yields. The nut is high in complex carbohydrates (an essential part of a healthy diet), and Africans actually prefer its taste to that of peanuts.

• *The Desert Date.* "In the Sudan alone," says the booklet, "there is a potential yield of 400,000 tons of fruit each year from the desert date tree, which can be processed to give edible oils, a substitute for peanuts, and animal feed." According to one estimate, every inhabitant of the Sahel region (an area in Africa where famine's touch is frequently felt) could obtain up to 450 kilograms (about a thousand pounds) of fruit and leaves from these local, wild trees each year."

• *The Hausa Potato.* This African tuber, all but unknown to scientists, is eaten by millions of Africans, and has great potential benefit to millions more. "Could go a long way toward relieving chronic food shortages in some of the driest parts of Africa."

- *"Hungry Rice."* (This plant's other name, *Digitaria exilis,* isn't quite as catchy.) The grain is eaten as a porridge, in soups, or as a side dish. Livestock can eat the leaves and seeds, and the dried plant makes good hay. "Hungry rice grows well in arid areas and on poor, sandy soils." It has a high nutritional value as well.

- *The Marama Bean.* Another legume that Noel Vietmeyer and the NAS say "has the potential to become a world-class crop." Below ground, it produces a large, edible tuber. Above ground, it's a vine (which is a nice bonus because it can be trellised to save home garden space) that produces nutritious, tasty seeds. "After roasting, the seeds have a nutty flavor that has been compared to that of cashew nuts."

- *Tamarind.* This tall, fruit-bearing tree is native to Africa, yet it is only cultivated currently in India; from there the fruit ("much in demand for use in sauces" such as Worcestershire) is exported all over the world. Surely, the land to which the tree is native should also get a piece of the potential cash crop action!

- *Teff.* Like amaranth, teff produces large quantities of small, high-protein seeds that are very well balanced in amino acid composition. Pancakes made from its fermented flour form the basic diet of millions of Ethiopians. "Teff seems to have ideal qualities as a grain crop for difficult, semi-arid climates . . . yet it is almost unknown outside Ethiopia."

- *Ye-eb.* This small, unattractively named bush "produces a nutritious and tasty nut with a chestnutlike flavor (and) survives in the fierce Ogaden Desert where rainfall is often less than six inches per year." Unfortunately, this valuable enemy of famine "is now so reduced by regional droughts, war and refugee concentrations that it is threatened with extinction."

That's a partial list. I can think of many other entries. The winged bean and moth bean of Asia spring to mind, as do grains such as quinoa from South America and our own, North American tepary bean.

Other people and ecologically minded organizations working along similar lines have begun to collect information about many more neglected native crops. And there are a *lot* of neglected native crops to study—hundreds of plants that could produce food, fodder, and (as we'll see in an upcoming chapter) fuel in the worst of times. Plants that could successfully defy famine.

And Africa, that once lush land, is still surprisingly rich with these valuable plants. The NAS-NRC report begins by pointing out there are:

> at least 2,000 indigenous food plants lying unappreciated in scattered parts of Africa.
>
> With this native botanical wealth, Africa can . . . improve the people's nutrition and increase their incomes. It can combat hunger using traditional resources. And it can build a sustainable agriculture for its future, not to mention contributing towards preserving the world's genetic diversity.

That last point is extremely important. We are all aware of the magnificent animals that face extinction. Yet many plants face the same threats, the same fate. And like animals, when they're gone, they're gone forever. Those plants—and others like them—contain the hope and promise of food and raw materials for all. But if they ever are to fulfill that promise, they first must be saved and studied.

Relief and development plans must change tactics. They must turn away from ill-considered imports and turn instead to these native plants, encouraging their cultivation once again.

In some areas, that will not be easy. People have been told for many years by the experts that their native plants were worthless. Only the strongest and smartest have refused to believe that—the ones who have survived the famines, the ones whose images we never saw because they never had to make the death march to the camps of despair. They remained on their small farms, tending their home gardens, and eating their famine plants.

Again, from the NAS-NRC report:

> It is paradoxical that although Africa is rich in native crops, the greater part of its agriculture relies on introduced crops. Nearly 90 percent of Sub-Saharan Africa's major food crops are foreign. Most originated in the Americas.

The report speaks of the badly needed pride that a return to native crops will provide to Africans. Both the Rodale Institute and the NAS and NRS hope that, with some explanation and apologies for previous campaigns designed to turn these people against their agricultural heritage, the return of true local food should be quickly accepted.

And the report again reminds us that these crops have the added benefit of coming complete with tolerance and resistance to local pests, resistance that is desperately needed. "Several of the major introduced crops are suffering devastating disease and pest outbreaks," NAS-NRC reports. A "broad array of backup substitutes" is necessary to stave off future disaster. As an example, the report cites the streak-virus epidemic that is attacking corn plants in West Africa (a version of the blight we mentioned previously that devastated the U.S. corn crop in the 1970s).

But the main advantage of famine plants will always be their innate ability to grow where nothing else can survive, their potential to allow people to literally farm the desert.

"In the future more and more Africans will have to depend on marginal lands for growing their food," says the NAS-NRC report. That's the hard reality of the Third World population explosion.

There's still plenty of land left, but all the good sites were taken long ago. In order to survive, people need to grow their food on areas unsuited to conventional agriculture. And we know that many of those neglected native crops can grow where the imported ones don't have a chance. Native plants really are the only realistic way to feed the rapidly expanding Third World population.

Rather than divert the water sources of the world to try to irrigate the desert (a tactic that just doesn't work for long, even in places where it initially seems successful) why not just grow plants that can survive without much water? The desert will become green again—naturally. The survival of crops will hold sand in place. Rotting vegetable matter will slowly turn that sand to soil. More plants will hold more sand in place, creating even more soil until the desert's harsh expansion has halted.

The better soil will allow less hardy crops to survive as well. Eventually, there will be enough roots in that soil to protect it from flash floods and harsh winds: one less piece of desert. One more little piece of green and fertile land.

The NAS-NRC report also notes that, as with amaranth, the cash value of many famine plant crops can be substantial. On the other hand, the value of the overplanted cash crops that are grown now (when they manage to survive) is dubious at best. Many experts feel that developing nations have a better chance to pay off their debts with profits from famine plants than they do with corn and coffee and cotton.

Over and over again, a convincing argument can be made that these neglected native plants are a key solution for a world in trouble. Yet these plants have been pushed to the side by experts intent on planting super-corns and super-rices; neglected by governments trying desperately to pay their debts with cotton and coffee at the expense of their people's health. These famine plants, these indigenous crops, these locally rooted survivors of the worst that nature can throw their way are essential to our plan for famine prevention.

We're not proposing a massive all-or-nothing change. People can still grow some corn. But when the corn dies from lack of rain, or when there isn't fertilizer to spare, or when disease or insects attack, the amaranth will be there. And the teff. And the winged bean. And the groundnuts.

No one need go hungry.

And just allow yourself to contemplate for a moment the wonderful side effect that encouraging the growth of these native plants will have: The desert will shrink.

I believe that one reason why the desert has so prospered in recent years has been the gradual loss of these native plants. After all, one of their main functions in the ecological balance has been simply to survive on the edge—or sometimes right smack in the middle—of desert and to stabilize the land. With living roots, they hold sandy soil in place and drink up the occasional rains. (One desert tree we will speak of later doesn't even need rains—it survives on the mists that cloud the desert at dawn.)

More foliage, less desert. Slowly, even the greenhouse effect itself will be challenged by such a simple change. The entire environment—including ours here in North America—will benefit (unless, of course, you were looking forward to more record heat waves in the future).

That positive change will come from two directions. Growing native plants (unlike corn and other plantation crops) doesn't require fossil fuel or petroleum-based fertilizers. So substituting them for current crops will limit the harmful emissions that fuel the greenhouse effect. And, of course, the addition of green, growing plants (that don't die every time the rains are late) will add badly needed oxygen to the atmosphere.

Almost every city in the United States is now planting trees to offset the greenhouse effect. Just think of the added benefits that re-claiming a continent's worth of desert could achieve! Fewer harm-ful emissions. More green cover to cool the earth. Slowly the balance will shift. And it must, for the growth of the desert threat-ens us all.

The reflective surface of the growing deserts of the world has meant a warmer world for us all. And many experts feel that the lo-cal effect of the desert's spread in Africa has prevented cloud for-mation, forestalled rains, and thereby extended the droughts. Droughts that, of course, help the desert to grow even more.

Locally, more plants may in themselves mean more rains. The famine plants could turn things around so well that they could practically put themselves out of business (though we should never allow that to happen again). Combined with our firewood solution (see Chapter 6), they have the potential to make Africa green again. To restore the continent to something more like the stories of years ago—to once again make it the lushest land in the world.

Globally, the return of native plants to developing nations will help us all breathe easier. A simple change of agricultural tactics has the potential to put into motion a series of events that can help us save our world.

CHAPTER SIX

Firewood That Feeds the World: The Miracle of Alley Cropping

As we said back in Part One, the face of Africa has changed greatly over the years. Much of the lushest land the world has ever seen has been eroded away to become desert.

Have I given the impression so far that the plantations of corn, cotton, coffee, and similar crops that replaced the traditional home gardens are the *only* reasons this destruction of the land has occurred? Those crops are certainly responsible for much of the desert's growth. Both directly—by draining the soil of its nutrients and then leaving it barren and at the mercy of wind and rain—and indirectly as well.

Some of the food grown on those plantations has itself led to a heavy demand on one of Africa's chief allies in holding back the desert—trees. Unlike the traditional crops it replaced, corn requires a lot of cooking—a lot of heat. A lot of wood. And, as we also said earlier, corn caused much indirect damage simply by fueling a massive population explosion. The sheer numbers of that corn-fed population have had an incredible impact on local trees.

In Africa, wood is needed for almost everything: building materials, plant stakes, crafts—and, of course, firewood and charcoal. When the plantation-fed population grew so rapidly, forested land was cleared much faster than the trees could possibly be replaced. And that loss of tree cover has been the desert's strongest ally.

Don't get me wrong, crops—especially the tough, local famine plant varieties—do a great job of holding fragile, vulnerable soil in place. But nothing does the job like a tree. Trees protect hillsides by holding the land's most fragile, easily movable soil in place. Tree roots soak up heavy rains with greater efficiency than any other type of plant life can. With healthy trees poised to take advantage of tropical rains, hillside runoff is reduced to a trickle instead of a torrent.

The most recent haunting images of hunger to invade our living rooms have left us equating famine with dust, drought, and deserts. The latest famines have been the result not just of war, poor agricultural choices, and debt, but of lack of rains. The most recent famines we've seen have been in sub-Saharan Africa, where rainfall has always been slim and unpredictable—a situation only made worse by the expansion of the desert. (As we mentioned before, allowing a desert to expand is felt by most experts to have the disastrous side effect of decreasing the total amount of rainfall in that area. In that light, deserts themselves appear to be highly efficient entities. Their growth creates conditions—specifically a decline in rainfall—that in turn accelerates that growth even faster. It's a nasty cycle.)

But famines have many beginnings, and can be caused by floods as well as by lack of moisture. The last big famine in Bangladesh, for example, was associated with floods. And even when famine is not a result, the flooding associated with forest depletion can still cause a devastating loss of life.

In *Food and the Environment* (1989, a World Food Day publication), the FAO (the Food and Agriculture Organization) provides a startling look at just how many lives we're talking about. In comparison, famine's toll seems almost restrained. The FAO recounts that

> Every year, at least 11 million hectares (around 28 million acres) of tropical forest are cut down. The consequences are devastating. Vital watersheds . . . are stripped, exposing the soil to erosion and increasing the risk and volume of floods.
>
> In the 1960s, there were 5.2 million flood victims every year; in the 1970s, the number tripled.

That's a simple, but horrifying equation: As more trees are cut down by hungry people looking for wood, increasing millions of the world's children die from hunger or the hideous effects of uncontrolled floods, every year.

Big floods almost invariably increase the local people's vulnerability to famine. Crops, people, and entire villages are simply swept away by raging waters. The land itself is drowned.

But in Africa, the famine-causing floods are small, local, and seasonal. They are the floods of sudden tropical rainstorms that can strip a treeless mountain of its soil in a few hours. Floods of runaway rainwater that loosen and carry rocks, boulders, and stones to the land below.

Picture a field of crops that might be able to survive a torrent of sudden rain alone, now having to also cope with virtual rivers of mud pouring down from nearby hillsides as well. The crops are buried by mud, crushed by stones and rocks, or simply drowned by all the water. So you see, too much rain in too short a period of time can be as bad as no rain at all. Especially when there are no trees to help lessen the impact of a sudden tropical deluge.

The lack of trees also has an effect on the wells in the area. When trees are lost, wells dry up rapidly. Normally, wells are filled when rainwater soaks slowly through the soil and down into the well. But on eroded hillsides, rainwater doesn't soak in—it runs off. The wells begin to dry up. A bad situation only gets worse—all because of the loss of trees.

My hope is that, by implementing the changes that I and many others feel have the potential to lessen the threat of famine in Africa, the desert's spread will slowly be brought to a halt. After being halted, that spread can be reversed.

The desert is winning right now because the wrong plants are at the edge. Let's put the right plants at the edge and move things in the other direction. As that welcome change occurs, more moisture will be available to condense into clouds. Rainfall will become more plentiful. Those rains may even return to a more predictable pattern as well.

Part of this greening of the desert will be achieved by replacing plantations with home gardens. Gardens containing the kinds of native crops that can not only survive but thrive in those areas on the edge, still unclaimed by the desert's sandy fingers. But no solution will work unless it protects the last of the wooded hillsides. Any realistic plan for famine prevention in Africa must also include a way to stop those long, dusty marches for firewood that so please the desert.

The problems caused by firewood gathering have not been totally missed by the experts. In fact, much effort has gone into developing ways to slow Africa's rapid deforestation.

Unfortunately, most of the response has been in the form of a development technique known as "appropriate technology." The solution that's been attempted on the largest scale so far has been to try to sell the native people efficient stoves, so that less wood is used for cooking.

That can be a partial solution to the problem where stoves are perceived as culturally acceptable. In fact, programs selling such improved stoves have achieved some success in areas where the people were already stove users (as some tribes in Africa are) and where the people have the money to buy the new stoves. But the vast majority of Africans do not have the money. And this solution, like so many others conceived by experts abroad, ignores the cultural and spiritual needs of many of the people it purports to assist. If those experts would spend a bit more "hut time," as I call it, they would learn that to many Africans, stoves are simply seen as undesirable.

The stoves don't give off enough light or heat to chase away the nighttime dark and chill. There is not enough smoke released to kill the bugs in the thatched roof or to keep away the often deadly mosquitos. The stoves don't provide the entertainment, the almost indescribable sense of enjoyment provided by an open fire.

I simply don't think it's right to go into another culture with a lot of solutions that don't take into account the wants, needs, and lifestyle of the people you're supposed to be helping.

It's also unnecessary. The Africans themselves already have the solution to their firewood problem—it's firmly rooted in their own past. And again, that solution is to be found in the centuries-old traditional home garden-farm system.

But, due to the emergency nature of the situation, the solution we (and other, similarly minded groups) propose is slightly improved and more efficient than the old way.

Although African home gardens were—at least to Western eyes—disorganized and random in appearance, they managed to contain everything necessary to sustain life in rural areas with unpredictable (and often inhospitable) climates. And one of their most valuable components was a wonderful family of trees that are legumes.

Legumes are a very distinctive variety of plant life. I won't go into all the characteristics of legumes here, but the term encompasses a wide variety of species, including ground covers (like clover), peanuts, most types of beans (including the extremely versatile soybean)—and trees. Wonderful trees. As we mentioned earlier in the book, legumes "fix" nitrogen. Nodules within their roots contain naturally occurring bacteria that allow them to literally pull this essential plant-growing nutrient out of the air.

Agricultural scientists have long felt that plants growing near legumes received free nitrogen that was transferred underground by the root systems. Lately, some people suspect that this may not be the case after all. The whole subject is currently a matter of great dispute.

But there is no dispute about the fertilizing value of the legumes themselves. The actual plant material—the leaves and branches of leguminous growth—is a rich source of nitrogen and other essential plant nutrients.

There are many ways to use this free fertilizer. One popular organic gardening-farming technique is to grow a leguminous ground cover such as clover, and then plow all the plants into the soil to enrich and fertilize the earth naturally. Or you can just spread the leaves and other plant material around the base of your crops and the nitrogen and other nutrients will be released slowly over a period of time. Natural, time-released plant food. In Africa, the tremendous amount of fertilizer produced by fast-growing leguminous trees could be the central element of a user-friendly, ecologically sound growing system—alley cropping—that truly deserves to be called "sustainable agriculture."

In a moment I'll delve into my research material and present some startling numbers that illustrate very specifically just how beneficial leguminous trees are. But before that, a bit of a general explanation.

In Africa, the rural people are the ones who are most at risk of famine. Governments tend to feed the people in the cities—often at the expense of the rural poor—because they fear that people in concentrated urban areas present a greater threat in the form of a potential revolution against the established order.

The needs of the rural people are simple needs—obtaining enough food and firewood. Because of reasons that include (but are certainly not limited to) political instability and lack of roads, it is difficult, if not impossible, to import things like fertilizer to help them achieve that goal.

But such expensive and ecologically unsound imports really are unnecessary. Untold centuries ago, the home garden evolved to supply all the needs of rural Africans. A mixture of native plants and leguminous trees, these combination garden-farms can provide a family with all it needs.

Alley cropping simply takes the ancient idea of the home garden and makes it more efficient. In an alley-cropping system, rows of fast-growing leguminous trees are planted, with room between the rows for native plants (or other crops). You start with foot-high seedlings, so the crops nearby grow unshaded (perhaps receiving nitrogen from the nearby leguminous roots).

As the trees grow, they are constantly cut back, according to the season. If the foods crops nearby need more sun, the trees are cropped closely. If shade is needed, the trees are left to grow.

And once they are cut (five times a year is the norm), the only problem is deciding what to do with those cuttings. The choices are almost endless. The leaves and small branches make a great combination mulch-fertilizer for the growing crops surrounding the trees. Applied in heaping piles around the base of food-producing plants, this nutritious litter acts as a wonderful cooling mulch. The piles of leaves shade the ground, keeping the sun from drying out the soil. And as the leaves decompose, they release natural nitrogen—fertilizer that (unlike its mass-produced, chemical-based equivalent) doesn't burn sensitive young plants and poses no runoff threat to pollute the local water supply or nearby lakes and streams.

Nitrogen is the single most essential nutrient for plant life. And also the one most lacking in tropical soils. Even the normally conservative U.S. Department of Agriculture points out (in a 1980 manual, *Techniques and Plants for the Tropical Subsistence Farm*) that "there is little nitrogen available in tropical soils" and that the best source for this essential nutrient is the compost of leguminous plants.

The leaves of many leguminous trees also make excellent animal feed. Having a variety of small animals (for milk and meat) is also a traditional component of the African home garden system. And, of course, the trees are a rich source of firewood. I'll quote some astounding statistics shortly, but to put it simply, many of those trees grow very rapidly and can be cut back to a virtual stump without any harm to the tree itself.

When the trees begin to shade the crops underneath, you cut them back fiercely and then divvy up the spoils. The larger branches (and maybe even the top of the trunk) for firewood, plant stakes, and building materials. Smaller branches for kindling. Leaves for fertilizer, animal food, and food for people.

Yes, people.

What the experts don't know is that people eat the trees of Africa. On the day I learned this remarkable fact, my friend Bede Okigbo and I were talking about the damage done to an area's soil when trees disappear on nearby hillsides. Okigbo is the director of the Program on Natural Resources in Africa, of the U.N. University Office in North America. So he has a special interest in the problem. He mentioned that he thought the situation caused by loss of trees was even worse in his native Nigeria, despite the fact that most of the area was fairly level, because the trees provided food for the people there as well.

I said, "Oh, you mean because they're legumes that fix nitrogen and provide fertilizer to grow food crops."

But he told me no—Nigerians actually *eat* the leaves of twenty-two different trees! Now, that seemed very strange to me—I had never heard of such a thing! I asked him, "Do they eat them raw or cooked?" He explained that a certain number are eaten raw and others need to be cooked. We talked about it for a while, and I left feeling that I had really learned something.

A few weeks later, I was visiting with a leading agricultural expert in East Africa—a cocky Englishman with a degree who had actually done some farming in Africa himself. I asked him, "Did you know that in Nigeria people eat the leaves of trees?"

And he said, "No. I never heard of that."

Now here is a man who is relied on by the top development people to set agricultural policy and he doesn't know that Nigerians eat the leaves of twenty-two different trees! That's why we in the famine-fighting business need to stay in touch with people like Okigbo—true experts who know the history and culture of the area, who know what the people at risk of famine really do and really eat.

In a later conversation, Okigbo explained to me that not only do Nigerians eat those leaves, but that the food—and sometimes medicine—produced by native trees is very important to them. He feels (and I have come to agree) that the importance of trees to the Nigerian food supply simply can't be overemphasized. And that's true for the rest of Africa as well. Even where people don't eat their leaves, trees provide such a variety of services that I doubt even this chapter will touch on them all.

One such benefit is the shade the trees provide if cutting is delayed. The shade that protects the alley-cropped plants underneath from the scorching sun, allowing those plants to survive long droughts.

(My editor tells me that he uses trees this way in his own garden—to keep his lettuce, peas, and spinach from bolting in the summer.)

The list of usable items provided by leguminous trees is startling: high-nitrogen fertilizer, twigs and sticks for crafts and kindling, food for humans, food for animals, stakes, firewood, building materials, medicine—even, as we'll see in a later chapter—a natural insecticide.

Thus the food production in Africa is tied very intimately to trees.

Now I want to present the case for alley cropping. The information in this section (unless otherwise noted) comes from *Alley Cropping: A Stable Alternative to Shifting Cultivation* (1988), a booklet prepared by the International Institute of Tropical Agriculture (IITA), the people who coined the term "alley cropping" and who have done the most to document its effectiveness.

The giant leguminous tree known as *Leucaena leucocephala* (everybody just calls it Leucaena, pronounced "Loo-Kayna") produces enormous amounts of fertilizer-rich cuttings. In tests, "a well-established hedgerow" planted in sandy soil and pruned five times a year produced fifteen to twenty tons of fresh prunings per hectare per year. (The metric unit hectare equals about two-and-a-half acres.) That impressive amount of green material ultimately yielded between five and six and a half tons of dry organic matter, rich in fertilizing nutrients.

After the stake-sized limbs were removed for plant supports and firewood, the dried prunings of one hectare provided over 350 pounds of nitrogen, 33 pounds of phosphorus, 330 pounds of potash, and respectable yields of cadmium and manganese—trace elements also necessary for healthy plant growth. That's a small fortune in free fertilizer. And, as we said earlier, it's fertilizer that won't harm the environment by polluting wells or causing excessive algae growth in streams and rivers the way chemical fertilizers do.

And the preceding figures are far from a record. In Hawaii one researcher growing Leucaena got well over a thousand pounds of fertilizing nitrogen from each 2.5-acre plot!

In an alley-cropping experiment in Nigeria, reported by Y. S. Chen and others in the journal *HortScience* (1989), fourteen months' worth of Leucaena prunings provided 490 pounds of nitrogen per hectare. In between the rows of trees were planted sweet (bell) peppers, chinese cabbage, amaranth, cucumber, cabbage, cowpea, broccoli, lettuce, and other vegetables.

Yields with Leucaena prunings were just as good as with conventional fertilizer application. (Actually, fresh-weight yields of at least one Leucaena-fed crop were double that obtained with chemicals!)

Soil erosion was well controlled in the cropped rows—but not in the chemically fertilized ones. With chemical cultivation, valuable (and irreplaceable) soil was lost.

And on top of all that, the researchers even note "the better growth appearance of the alley-cropped plants."

Back to the IITA booklet: The natural fertilizer produced by Leucaena does not require a long wait, either. The speedy production record might just belong to the researcher who managed to get more than 279 pounds of nitrogen by trimming a hectare of *four-month-old* Leucaena plants in Colombia!

And don't forget—all this free fertilizer is just the haul from leaves and small branches. The plants also contribute a lot of wood to the families who raise them. In a typical situation, fully grown Leucaena that had been planted in between rows of corn and cowpeas produced almost six tons of stakes per hectare per year. That's almost three tons of wood per acre without ever actually cutting down a tree!

Such astounding wood production is one of the most amazing benefits of these wonderful trees. Normally you have to kill a tree to get firewood. Even if you replant a seedling instantly to take its place, you still must wait ten or twenty years before that replacement tree is a good source of wood. But with Leucaena (and other fast-growing, firewood-appropriate leguminous trees) you just prune what you want and the rapidly growing tree instantly starts making more wood for you.

And the trees are incredibly drought resistant. The IITA reports that during the four-month-long dry season, Leucaena grew more than twelve feet—using subsoil moisture alone! "When allowed to grow uninhibited for one year," the IITA reports, "the Leucaena hedgerow easily reached a height of over 7.5 meters [about 25 feet] and produced more than 88 tons of wood per hectare."

Now that you have an idea of the sheer mass of essential resources that trees like Leucaena can provide, I'd like to jump back to the free fertilizer aspect. The IITA reports some exciting success stories in actual situations where prunings were used to fertilize fields. When Leucaena prunings were added to cornfields as the only fertilizer, yields jumped to as much as four tons per hectare. Commercial fertilizer could hardly have done better. In another experiment, corn yields doubled in both 1980 and 1981 (despite a severe drought that year), tripled in 1982, and increased by a factor of almost eight in 1983 when Leucaena prunings were retained on alley-cropped plots.

Those are not isolated examples. Many studies have shown Leucaena (and other leguminous tree) prunings to be an excellent natural source of nitrogen and other essential plant-growing nutrients, both by analysis and by demonstration on actual crops in the field.

And we're not just talking about corn. The nutrient content of various leguminous trees is excellent for growing a wide variety of crops. Besides those crops noted in the *HortScience* article quoted previously, success has been reported with cowpeas, rice, and root crops like yams.

Both Leucaena (the real "star" of the legume tree species) and another hedgerow species known as Gliricidia provide excellent high-protein fodder for livestock.

The amount of shrubbery produced by these trees in a home garden system has been shown to provide enough fodder to feed a typical number of farm animals (such as goats and sheep) during the dry season, when survival by grazing becomes difficult, if not totally impossible. And the trees provide that food without any irrigation, thanks to thirsty roots that seek water deep below the surface.

The IITA also points out a few other alley-cropping benefits I had failed to mention earlier. First, the mulch of the nutrient-rich leaves not only shades and cools the soil, but also kills weeds by depriving them of sunlight. "The suppression of weeds is . . . viewed as a major advantage of alley cropping," reports the IITA, "especially in small-scale farming where weeding can take more than 30 percent of the labor used in crop production."

Second, the breakdown of the decomposing leaves does more than just mulch and release fertilizer—it also adds organic matter back to the soil. The decaying leaves literally become additional soil for the garden (we'll discuss in Chapter 8 why this is vital). "Plots receiving prunings contained twice the amount of soil organic matter as plots where prunings were removed," reports the IITA.

And this decay, in combination with the soil-cooling action of the mulch, has an additional beneficial action as well. The rotting organic matter encourages the growth and vitality of organisms in the soil—from microbes and bacteria that fight disease and aid in plant growth all the way up to the earthworms that are every garden's friend. These beneficial organisms—essential to a healthy ecosystem—add extra nutrients and provide a better medium for growth to the plant that has been swathed in leguminous leaves.

When planted across the contours of a sloping field, hard-working leguminous trees create a living barrier that effectively traps soil and blocks rapid flows of rainwater. This combination controls erosion, literally creating a field out of an area once un-suited to farming.

Moreover, with a technique called live staking, you don't even have to trim the trees to get plant stakes! African natives long ago developed this method of using the growing limbs of the trees in their home gardens as living supports for vine crops and other climbing plants. (Think of it as growing pole beans in your own garden, only the trees are the poles!) And when the crop is har-vested, they can trim the living stakes for another use.

And the nitrogen fertilizer released from the alley crop prunings is kinder to the soil than its chemical equivalent. Chemical fertil-izers often provide short-term benefits and long-term problems, such as slowly increasing the acidity of the soil they (supposedly) enrich to the point where it can no longer support plant life. "Re-peated application of [conventional] nitrogen fertilizer increased soil acidity, but the addition of Leucaena prunings did not," re-ports the IITA.

You can get that nitrogen at the rate of release you want—the rate most appropriate to individual crops and your own needs at the time. Want it fast? Buried in the soil to aid decomposition, fresh Leucaena prunings released half their nitrogen content in less than 10 days! (Dried prunings decompose even faster.) Don't want that much that soon? Laid on the surface, the prunings release their ni-trogen much more slowly.

You just can't get that kind of a choice from conventional chem-ical fertilizers.

In its booklet, the IITA explains that the idea for alley cropping grew out of the ancient "bush fallow" method of traditional African agriculture. Basically, that term refers to a technique we described earlier, where land is cultivated for a period of time and then abandoned—allowed to "return to the bush," as they say in Africa. "This fallow restores soil fertility and rids the land of many noxious weeds, pests and diseases," says the IITA.

But, as we also said, population pressures and loss of good land to the desert have made the old bush fallow system an impossible dream for most Africans. Today, if you have access to land that can support cultivation, you are pretty much forced by circumstances to keep it in constant use.

That means finding ways to farm the same piece of land year after year. In the United States, that's mostly achieved through the use of chemicals and heavy equipment (which is why I strongly feel that we too are courting famine by our farming methods).

As the IITA explains:

> Fragile tropical soils do not respond well to temperate farming methods based on the use of heavy machinery and expensive agrochemicals, which often leave the land in poorer condition than does a heavily used bush fallow system.
>
> In an attempt to incorporate the good features of bush fallow into a continuously productive farming system, scientists at IITA have developed a production system for tropical agriculture called alley cropping . . . growing food crops in alleys formed by leguminous trees or shrubs.

To its credit (and probably ensuring its remarkable success with the technique over the years), the IITA never forgot the bush fallow origin of its research:

> The restorative power of the bush fallow is linked to the regrowth of deep rooted trees and shrubs that recycle plant nutrients and build up soil organic matter.

During the fallow period, plant cover and litter protect the soil from the impact of high intensity raindrops and the roots help to bind the soils, increase water infiltration and reduce runoff and soil erosion.

Moreover, litter mulch and shading by tree and shrub canopies reduce soil temperature and maintain soil moisture conditions that are favorable for the growth of beneficial organisms.

In addition to restoring soil fertility, the bush fallow provides supplemental food, animal feed, staking material, firewood and herbal medicine.

I feel especially good about repeating this IITA summary of alley cropping's bush fallow roots. And not only because its theme—the rediscovery of ancient Africa's coping strategies to prevent future famines—is so in line with our own. It turns out that the section on alley cropping's bush origin is followed by a reference, indicating that the IITA is quoting someone else's work. Being quoted is my good friend Bede Okigbo, who appears to have influenced many minds with his invaluable knowledge of Africa's fertile past. (And who, by the way, is currently writing a new book on the benefits of the African home garden system for the Rodale Institute.)

By now you've probably figured out that our famine prevention plan also incorporates alley cropping of leguminous trees as part of the reintroduction of the home gardens that we feel has the potential to forestall famine. And, of course, you're correct.

But you would be wrong if you assumed we propose to use only the Leucaena variety of leguminous tree. Unlike the developers, we have learned the lesson of the Green Revolution—namely, never depend on any one single species, no matter how perfect or superior it seems. We propose a variety of leguminous trees in every home garden. Otherwise, we would risk inviting disease and pest attacks in the same way as those experts who planted vast areas with single species of vulnerable food crops.

One of the first things that I decided as I saw the benefits of Leucaena demonstrated over and over again was not to be swayed by its success. There are many varieties of leguminous trees, each with their own strong points and individual features. An entire family, known collectively as the *acacias,* contains many individual species well known for their ability to provide high-quality animal fodder in the world's deserts. Other trees and shrubs being researched for use in alley cropping include *Calliandra calothyrsus,* which may produce the most firewood in the shortest period of time, and *Acioa barterii,* whose leaves provide the slowest-decomposing fertilizer of any variety studied thus far.

And one tree—of whose existence I have only recently become aware—appears to be even more drought resistant than the deep drinkers that survive the African dry season with deep roots that drink up sub-soil moisture. This tree, *Prosopis cineraria,* surviving in the driest and hottest of deserts, is also a deep drinker. But when there is no deep water to drink, it seems able to survive on dew—on the moisture provided by the desert's morning mists.

In his book *The Sea of Sands and Mists,* Nigel Winser recounts his experiences as part of a group mapping the life in the Wahiba Sands for Britain's Royal Geographic Society. The Wahiba Sands lie in the Arabic nations just across the slim strait of the Red Sea from Africa. In fact, the desert Winser writes about, "an area hardly mentioned in literature and which was described in the local geographical textbooks as an 'inhospitable place where no one lives,'" is very close in latitude to Africa's Sudan region.

And those books, he recounts, are wrong. Rather than the area being uninhabited and inhospitable, he and his colleagues discovered that "over 3,000 nomadic Bedu make it their home." As these desert dwellers told the researchers, "we *choose* to live here." And so does a wide variety of other life. Life that, properly studied, has great potential to help control the spread of desert on the other side of the Red Sea.

The average rainfall in the Sands is believed to be less than ten millimeters a year. Not enough to sustain life as we know it. And yet the Royal Geographers discovered enough new plants to bring the desert's known total up to 176. "Far in excess of what we had hoped for," recounts Winser, who adds that "they [the number of plants that survive in the Sands] gave confidence to all who believe that all deserts can one day be turned green."

But the star of the desert landscape is surely the tree known as *Prosopis cineraria*. Winser points out that, although different varieties of Prosopis are distributed worldwide, "growing in the harshest environments," this particular variety is not known outside of Iran, Afghanistan, and the Arabian peninsula.

"It shows a lot of variation in shape and structure," he reports. "It can be a substantial oak-like tree up to 9 meters high or a bush only 1 meter high." But he suggests that the difference is not a natural one. The bush shape, he feels, may be the tree's forced adaption to constant trimming back by the natives, who make good use of its valuable wood.

Winser writes wonderfully of the tree's hardiness, "its capacity for vegetative regeneration, which enables it to survive severe cutting. . . ." As described by Winser, Prosopis sounds like an incredible resource: "It has a thick fissured grey bark and a heavy hard wood of high caloric value which is valued as firewood and as building material."

And, of course, it's a legume.

But back to the mists: Prosopis's main water-seeking strategy consists of growing deep tap roots that can reach almost 100 feet down in search of deeply buried moisture. However, this ability, recounts Winser, "still doesn't explain how the odd Prosopis survives in the middle of the sand when the watertable is over 150 feet down." He explains, "Remarkably, it appears that the Prosopis trees, like other desert plants, have the ability to absorb the night mists directly through the stomata, or pores, in the leaves once the dew has settled." Researchers in the group who worked at recording this dew found that (unlike on other surfaces) little was to be found on the Prosopis leaves in the morning, "presumably because it was now all safely drawn inside. This must be useful both when the tree is young and the tap root is relatively short and when it hasn't rained for awhile."

Another unique aspect of this tree is its ability to remain alive in greatly shifting sands that can deposit mounds many feet high in one blinding sandstorm. The tree achieves this miracle of survival simply by its ability to grow higher than the dunes that swallow up lesser trees. The Royal Geographers note that some of the trees' trunks were buried in twelve to fifteen feet of sand, yet their canopies had grown more than an additional sixty feet above the sands. A spectacular tree; a worthy adversary of the desert.

"Given the right conditions," says Winser, "Prosopis, colloquially known as *ghaf,* is a strong candidate for the [reforestation] of the arid and semi-arid areas which now cover one-third of the world's land surface and which are increasing by 5 million hectares [12.5 million acres] each year." He says that he had to sleep under Prosopis trees at night and take refuge from the desert's blazing heat under their sheltering leaves in the harsh daytime to "appreciate how very substantial they are. . . . The trees provide this badly needed shelter, wood for cooking, timber for huts, food in the form of edible fruit and leaves and fodder for livestock."

Winser hopes that the work of the Royal Geographic team will "put this remarkable tree (known to the natives as the 'Omani tree of life') at the forefront . . . [as] an effective plant for curbing the spread of desertification." He also calls for more research on the possibility of transferring this rugged hardwood to other harsh desert areas. Follow-up work, he calls it.

I agree. I'd like to see how some of these "trees of life" fare alongside the Leucaena and acacias and other leguminous trees in African home gardens. The combination promises to be a nearly invincible weapon against the desert; against famine and poverty. The least-vulnerable garden-farm will contain a mix of trees, a mix of crops, and a mix of multipurpose animals (for meat, milk, fertilizing dung, and power to pull plows). And by ensuring a mix of each essential ingredient, we can achieve great things—simply by not repeating the mistakes of the past twenty years and counting too much on any one star performer.

Simplicity. Smallness. Diversity. Appropriateness. Can I mention one more benefit of these wonderful trees? Dung. Sorry, but animal dung is one of the finest nutrients you can add to the soil. Have you ever seen dried, aged manure? It is soil, the finest earth there is—black, rich dirt that fairly hungers for seedlings to absorb its nutrients.

Yet in many famine-prone societies, dung is burned for fuel because the nearest firewood is many days away. In a 1988 publication, co-produced by the Environmental Policy Institute and the National Wildlife Federation, Walter Reid and his co-authors estimate that "400 million tons of dung are burned each year in lieu of fuelwood."

Dung does make fairly good fuel, but I feel it is wasted as such. Dung's true path lies in soil enrichment. As that same publication goes on to say, "the loss of this fertilizer source depresses annual grain harvests by some 20 million tons—enough to feed 100 million people for a year." And by combining the very different nutrients you get from leguminous leaves and from animal dung you get fertilizer capable of growing even more than that enormous amount. Capable of growing just about anything. Establishing row after row of leguminous trees to free up that valuable dung, save it from the fire, and allow it to go back where it belongs—to the earth. To feed millions of hungry people.

And the trees themselves will help ease the greenhouse effect. Your efforts to ease famine in Africa, in Mexico, and wherever people are vulnerable to its effects, will thus have an immediate effect on us as well. Ultimately, our summers will be cooler. Our air-conditioning bills will be lower. (Which means we'll be releasing less freon and other refrigerants into the atmosphere, which will also reduce the greenhouse effect!)

Part Two of the Rodale plan for famine prevention: Millions of seedlings. Research into different varieties. Volunteers assuring native people that it really is O.K. to go back to the old ways. Trees for Africa. Very special trees. Because food alone just isn't enough. We have to keep those spiritual fires burning.

CHAPTER SEVEN

Killing Pests
Without Poisons

I would hope that, by now, most people have been convinced of the need to reduce the use of toxic chemicals on food crops. Chemical fertilizers are one large area of concern. The other, better known chemicals are the "—cides."

Pesticides. Herbicides. Insecticides. Fungicides. Rodenticides. People have finally come to realize that if they want to avoid *sui*-cide, and quite possibly genocide, they need to get these other "—cides" out of their lives.

Unfortunately, there is a multibillion-dollar business ($8 billion a year in chemical fertilizer alone, says *The New York Times*) in making these things. So, as soon as you talk about farming without chemicals the political cry of "jobs" goes up immediately: "How dare you try to limit these incredibly toxic, dangerous substances? Don't you know that you'll just be putting Americans out of work?"

That's not how the chemical makers actually phrase their argument, of course. They maintain—like the cigarette manufactur-ers, who can keep a straight face while insisting that there is no proven link between their product and any kind of disease at all—that agricultural chemicals are actually safe.

I was stunned to see a chemical company representative on a network news show claim that pesticide-sprayed fruit was much safer than the organically grown variety! He stated with great assurance that organic fruit was tainted with some sort of disease left behind by the insects who had feasted on it, and he would never touch the stuff! Just amazing. Of course, he never actually named any of those imaginary diseases. Even worse, the moderator of the program never challenged him on this so-called fact.

Despite similar debating tactics by the tobacco industry, every medical organization on earth has assured us that cigarettes are the single biggest cause of preventable health problems and premature death in the world today. I firmly believe that agricultural chemicals are close behind. And, like cigarettes, the harm from such chemicals isn't confined to those who use them intentionally.

I'm talking about a different kind of "sidestream smoke," the secondhand exposure of millions of people to agricultural chemicals via massive pollution of wells and waterways. This pollution may even be more harmful than the damage those chemicals directly cause to agricultural workers who apply them and to people who eat produce laden with their residues. Unfortunately, corporate thinking in this country often seems to be rooted in the denial of risks, not their honest assessment and correction.

I believe that agricultural chemicals present an unnecessary risk, both here and in the Third World. They present a totally unacceptable risk to farmers and field workers who are exposed to these toxic chemicals in concentrations hundreds of times higher than those of us who simply eat some along with our supermarket fruits and vegetables.

They present a totally unacceptable risk to the world's water as well. Pesticides have been found in drinking water throughout the country. Much of the water in our nation's farming areas is heavily polluted with chemical fertilizer runoff. Because of that runoff, well water near farms often contains high levels of nitrates, substances strongly linked with cancer. Lakes and streams turn a hideous, sickly green when the same runoff fertilizes their aquatic plant life, causing it to grow beyond all bounds of nature. Fish, starved for oxygen in this sea of green, die in massive numbers.

My feeling—make that my *fear*—is that the pollution caused by agricultural chemicals is not known to nearly enough Americans. I don't think the water problems caused by these chemicals have hit home and really touched the public consciousness. Yet.

But thanks to a lucky near-tragedy, the same cannot be said for another negative effect of pesticides. All Americans are aware of at least one of the many tragic effects that pesticide use can have on wildlife. That's because one of the bird species hit hardest by the eggshell-thinning effect of DDT was our own American bald eagle.

I still have to wonder, though, if DDT might not still be on the market today if the birds whose eggshells it thinned had not included our national symbol. It shouldn't take the near-extinction of such a symbol to move people to action. Many more birds—some of whom, ironically, fulfill their part in the food chain by eating huge numbers of destructive insects—are still threatened by pesticide use today.

Even science now agrees that chemicals are unnecessary. Right up at the top of the front page of *The New York Times* for Friday, September 8, 1989, was a headline I had been waiting twenty years to see: "Science Academy Says Chemicals Do Not Necessarily Increase Crops; Policy Shift Urged to Discourage Pesticides." The first paragraph of the story says it all:

> The National Academy of Sciences has found that farmers who apply little or no chemicals to crops are usually as productive as those

who use pesticides and synthetic fertilizers, and today recommended changing Federal subsidy programs that encourage use of agricultural chemicals.

That last part is important. As the *Times* reports later in the story, "since the end of World War II, farmers have been taught by agricultural universities and the Department of Agriculture that the best way to increase output is to use ample amounts of chemical fertilizer and then protect the harvest with generous applications of pesticides." This, explains the *Times* article, results in huge surpluses that the government must then buy from the farmer. (Are you ready?) "This year [1989], farm subsidies cost the government $13.9 billion," reports the *Times*.

Yes, that's billion with a *B*. And, of course, this subsidy of well-poisoning chemicals doesn't really cost the government anything. After all, this is the United States. *We*—you and I—are the government. Those subsidies to overproduce come right out of our pockets at tax time. In a sense, *we* buy the pesticides that destroy wildlife and threaten our health through residues in drinking water and throughout the food chain. *We* pay for the fertilizer that's ruining our water supply and killing our lakes and streams.

Forgive me for straying for so long from Africa and the other parts of the Third World threatened by famine.

We will soon discuss the many chemical-free ways that pests can be controlled in the Third World. But first I just had to point out that there is—finally—strong, independent, scientific evidence for chemical-free farming. Because after they've made their argument about preserving jobs, the chemical producers' next strategy is to claim that a cease-fire in their chemical war against nature would lead to massive starvation.

We here at Rodale (both the Rodale Press and the independent, nonprofit Rodale Institute) have known for years that isn't true. Our experimental farms have shown time and time again what the

NAS recently announced—that you can grow and harvest ample amounts of safe, nutritious, good-looking foods without any chemicals at all. And our *New Farm* program has shown that the U.S. farmer can make even more money with an "organic" program than with one that relies on chemicals. (Those chemicals, after all, are expensive!)

My apologies, but in this chapter, I think we have to break our "keep it international" focus and bounce back and forth between the United States and the Third World. America, to show why chemicals must be avoided. The Third World, to show how they easily can be avoided—replaced by natural means.

Only by fully understanding the harm that chemicals have done here in the United States can we truly see the foolish path we follow. And why it must stop, everywhere.

We've already shown how to avoid one big group of chemicals—artificial fertilizers—in the Third World. And that's by growing leguminous trees. Leguminous trees both provide natural fertilizer directly and free up animal manure for fertilization by providing firewood to burn in place of that manure.

Likewise, herbicides have been shown to be unnecessary as well. Weeds can be controlled simply by the mulching and shading that is an integral part of the alley-cropping system. And the elimination of plantation farming in favor of the mixed, home garden system will help halt the spread of nightmare weeds such as Striga.

That leaves insects. And if there's anything we've learned to do especially well here at the home of *Organic Gardening* magazine, it's to eliminate destructive insects without the use of chemicals. In fact, one thing we've learned over the years is that you probably can't control destructive insects until you stop using chemicals.

In fact, it would be difficult to do a worse job than with pesticides. Here's a nice little *Harper's Index* statistic (from the June 1989 issue) for you:

• Percentage change, since 1945, in the amount of insecticide used on U.S. crops: Plus 900%

• Percentage change, since 1945, in the portion of U.S. crops lost to insects: Plus 86%

It would be nice if we could save the poor farmers of the Third World from that type of progress. But we'll have to work fast. Between 1964 and 1974 alone, pesticide use in Africa increased by a factor of ten. The same is true in other underdeveloped regions, where the Conservation Foundation reports that "acute and chronic pesticide poisoning are considered . . . pervasive problems."

And the results in decreased harvests can be devastating. The following examples come from The National Wildlife Federation.

Mexico's burgeoning cotton industry collapsed in the late 1960s when pests developed immunity to the synthetic insecticides that experts pressed farmers to rely on.

As mentioned earlier, one of the biggest failures of the Green Revolution occurred when pesticides were identified as the chief reason that the brown planthopper achieved the status of "the most serious rice pest in Asia" in the late 1970s. A graduate student from Berkeley, California, discovered that pesticides had so decimated the planthoppers' natural enemies that it was essentially freed from all predators. In both cases, pesticides worked hard to help the pest.

Rather than spray its natural enemies to death, our plan for planthopper control would be to make those enemies welcome and comfortable. That's a natural pest control technique for tropical Third World countries.

As we've mentioned before, it's difficult to translate U.S. farming experience into workable solutions for tropical Third World areas. There are just too many differences. And when you talk about insect pests in the Third World, the most important difference you have to take into account is the climate. Unlike most of the United States, there is no winter freeze in tropical areas such as Africa and Mexico. That means insects are a year-round problem. But it also means year-long life for the worst enemy of destructive pests: beneficial insects.

You already know of a few. Perhaps the best known is the praying mantis, an insect so overwhelmingly lethal to pests that it has the distinction of being protected by federal law. My editor in this endeavor, Mike McGrath, who is now the editor-in-chief of *Organic Gardening* magazine, as well, tells me that this protection gave these magnificent insects an almost mystical quality in his youth. Growing up in a row home in Philadelphia, he explains, not a summer would go by without the appearance of praying mantises on the screen door.

"Don't hurt them! You'll get arrested," the neighborhood children would say. Carefully, he explains, the revered insects would be carried to the nearest neighbor's summer tomato plants, supposedly there to stand guard and devour enemies of tomatoes.

But many other, lesser known insects perform similar functions. The common ladybug, for instance, has a voracious appetite for that most common and destructive garden pest, the plant-sapping aphid. The delicate-looking green lacewing is actually a tough bug killer, whose larval stage devours large numbers of aphids, mites, leafhoppers, thrips, and other pests.

And then there are the many varieties of such wasps as *Trichogramma*. Please don't confuse them with the giant, stinging wasps that send us running for cover in the summer. We're talking about wasps so tiny that they are almost invisible to our eyes. And they have no interest in humans whatsoever. These tiny predators seek only the eggs and field-stripping larvae of moths and butterflies. In nature's wonderful scheme of checks and balances, some of the farmer's most destructive foes are nothing more than food for Trichogramma's young.

Just one species of Trichogramma, first used deliberately by humans in 1960 against the destructive cotton bollworm, has been found to be an effective enemy of the larvae of some two to three hundred different moths and butterflies. And there are many other Trichogramma species already known and actively being bred. And Trichogramma is just one of several different types of beneficial wasps.

As many U.S. organic gardeners already know, all you have to do is release a batch of the tiny little wasps into your garden when caterpillars, cabbage worms, tomato hornworms, or other immature forms of moths and butterflies first appear.

Some wasps attack those early caterpillars, laying their eggs inside the beast. The caterpillar dies when the eggs hatch, releasing swarms of tiny caterpillar-killers, who finish off their host as they are born to the world. And each of those newly born wasps lives only to grow, go out and find another caterpillar, and lay its own eggs.

Other varieties of wasp prefer to attack and parasitize the eggs laid by the adult moth or butterfly. Instead of hatching a caterpillar, these eggs instead release the hungry Trichogramma who have taken their place inside. Once released, the young wasps seek out other caterpillar eggs to neutralize.

It's a magnificent display of what scientists call *biological control:* simply allowing one insect to do its job of feeding off another. One big advantage to the use of this technique in the Third World (where corn borers, the army worm, and cabbage-eating caterpillars are among the worst pests) is the tropical climate. The only disadvantage to predatory wasp use in most of the United States is that the wasps themselves are of tropical origin. They cannot survive the winter freeze and must be released in fresh numbers every season. But in the Third World, where there is no such freeze, the wasps multiply as long as there is food to sustain them.

Research by our own USDA has shown that the wasps simply die off if that food supply is ever exhausted. Their only reason for living is to use caterpillars and their eggs as hosts in which their young can incubate. No caterpillars, no more young. There is no danger of the wasps themselves ever moving on to harm anything beneficial.

Unfortunately, the prevailing attitude in the United States (and therefore, much of the world) is to continue to fight pests with inefficient chemicals. That attitude has greatly reduced the numbers of beneficial insects. Perhaps the least-known side effect of pesticide use is the harm that they have done to the balance of nature the world over. Time and time again it has been shown that these chemicals are rarely effective for very long in controlling the pests against which they are directed. But the chemicals are often all too effective and deadly against the beneficial insects (and birds, lizards, toads, frogs, and other efficient bug-eaters) who are out there trying to control those pests naturally.

Pesticides make it easy—for pests. From the FAO (*Food and the Environment*, 1989) comes this note:

> Instead of improving harvests, improper use of agrochemicals can actually reduce production. A dramatic case in point is the cotton-growing region of Nicaragua, where the extensive use of broad-spectrum pesticides over two decades killed so many natural predators that the number of economically important kinds of pests actually increased from five to nine. Yields decreased significantly. . . .
>
> The excessive use of pesticides may be a major cause of low crop yields, food contamination and environmental degradation in many parts of the world.

The FAO, "out of a recognition that the use of chemicals alone was not only ineffective but destructive," allied itself with another U.N. organization over fifteen years ago to promote the concept of integrated pest management internationally. Commonly known as IPM to organic gardeners and farmers, integrated pest management strategy emphasizes natural techniques such as crop rotation and use of beneficial insects as alternatives to chemical pest control.

It's nice to know that groups like the FAO recognized the need for change so long ago. But it's terribly disturbing to realize that—despite their interest and U.N. involvement—not nearly enough change has occurred between then and now. We have lost to pesticide poisoning untold billions of insects and birds whose entire purpose in life was to devour as many crop-eating insects as possible. That is a tragedy. A sad waste.

Here in the United States we could well be on the way to wiping out entire species of beneficial insects by indiscriminate spraying. And poisoning from pesticides has cut deeply into our bug-eating bird populations. All because the American Way seemed to say that not one bug could be tolerated.

The sad truth is that, with the U.S.-style chemical farming that's been exported to the Third World, crops generally aren't sprayed only in times of need. They're simply sprayed all the time. All season long.

As researchers from the Faculty of Agriculture, Forestry and Veterinary Science at the University of Dar es Salaam, working in cooperation with experts from our own Rodale Research Center, stated at a 1983 workshop on efficient farming techniques held in Tanzania:

> The [early] success achieved with synthetic insecticides . . . led to regular spraying programs on a routine, preventative basis . . . whether the pest was present in damaging numbers or not.
>
> But it also resulted in the development of resistance to various pesticides by many insect pests. Brown (1970) reported 119 insect species of agricultural importance to be resistant to insecticides, and today, some pests are practically immune to all available pesticides.

In addition, some secondary pests have become primary pests
because their natural enemies were killed by the insecticides in use.

To control resurgence of [these] pests, farmers have increased
applications of highly toxic insecticides. Under these circumstances, the cost of pest control often has made crop production
profitless, resulted in serious health hazards to agricultural workers
and deteriorated environmental quality.

And this destruction is all the sadder, because, as was pointed out at
that 1983 conference in Tanzania, "complete eradication [of pests]
is generally not needed for high yields. Most plant species can tolerate a certain level of damage without appreciable effect on vigor
and yield."

Such results aren't all that surprising if you think about it a bit.
Plants, insects, birds—even that often destructive life-form
known as the human being—were all created to live in a large and
varied ecosystem endowed with inborn, natural strategies to respond to threats.

Plants respond in at least two different ways to a minor insect
threat. Over generations they may develop new characteristics that
make them more resistant to attack by those pests. In the short run,
however, an insect attack simply signals the plants to grow faster
and stronger—apparently, to make up for any damage that the
bugs do. If there were no attack at all, the plants—living in a sterile,
unnatural environment—would get lazy. Their natural defenses
wouldn't kick in. Growth would be slow.

Isn't it a wonderful world we live in? Where plants respond to
insect pests by growing more food? Where every pest has a pest of
its own, and the most we may have to do to protect our food supply
is to identify and encourage those pests of pests? It's a world that
has no need for insecticides to ruin that wonderful alignment.

I can quote article after article if you like. They all make a good
case. The same case. Pesticides simply have never been a workable

long-term solution to pest control problems. No, pesticides are not a solution. They are the problem.

There is a wide variety of ways to deter and befuddle pests. Just about every agricultural expert who does not have some kind of a vested interest in pesticide production now agrees that reducing pesticide use would have a beneficial effect.

Birds would be spared to eat bugs. Beneficial insects would have a chance to get in there and do what they do best. And if insects could go generations without pesticide exposure, they might actually become vulnerable to those pesticides (used sparingly) once again. Without constant exposure making them stronger, destructive members of the insect kingdom should begin to lose their tolerance and resistance to pesticides.

And then, if pesticides were an appropriate way to meet a sudden, unexpected emergency, there's a chance they might actually work!

In the meantime, here are a few proven alternatives.

Repellant Plants

Our work at the Rodale Research Center has proven the merits of a technique known to many gardeners for generations: Interplanting food crops with certain (often aromatic) plants repels damaging insects and thus protects the crops. This seems to work in two ways. In some cases, the odor of the essential oil from the repellant plant (repellant only to insects by the way; the smell is often very pleasing to people) does actually repel insects that would otherwise feast on the food crop. In some other cases, however, the repellant plant simply masks the odor of the food crops nearby, and the insects can't locate the food by smell.

This is not just a short-term solution. If repellant plants were used on a massive-enough scale, there's every reason to believe that many insects would be unable to find food and would die hungry. The numbers of many pest species could be greatly reduced.

The results of field trials have shown that tansy and catnip are particularly effective against a variety of pests. But the full list of pest-repelling plants is a long one indeed. And every one is either edible or provides a marketable commodity as well. So when you grow one of these plants in your garden to repel pests, you're also planting something very worthwhile.

From the USDA, here's a partial list of some pests and the plants known to repel them:

Pest	Repellant Plant
Ants	Mint
Aphids	Mint, garlic, nasturtium
Cabbage butterfly	Mint, strong herbs
Potato beetle	Bean, eggplant
Corn earworm	Marigold
Cucumber beetle	Radish
Flea beetle	Mint, strong herbs, tomato
Leaf miner	Strong herbs
Bean beetle	Nasturtium
Squash bug	Nasturtium
Squash vine borer	Strong herbs
Weevils	Garlic
Whitefly	Nasturtium

The Mixed Garden

One of the benefits of a mixed cropping system ("polyculture versus monoculture," in agri-jargon) is a documented reduction in insect pest problems. In fact, many studies have shown that simply growing a variety of crops instead of just a single one in any given area is an extremely effective method of natural pest control. There are at least three reasons why. First, insects are confused by all the sights and smells and can't locate their host plant (that's the one they've grown to love to ravage). Second, insects are often repelled by the odor of at least one of the crops in the mix. Third, beneficial insects and other predators thrive in a mixed system, because it provides them with ideal places to live and hide. (That's why our own *Organic Gardening* magazine encourages readers not to remove all the weeds near or even inside their gardens. Small weedy areas greatly increase the chance of attracting and keeping beneficial predators nearby.)

Sadly, as was reported at the 1983 University of Dar es Salaam workshop in Tanzania, "although intercropping is as old as agriculture itself, modern farming in most countries means large acres of monoculture [one single crop] plantings. Consequently, insect pest problems arise." In East Africa, for instance, it has been shown on several occasions that simply planting beans and cowpeas in the same field with corn reduces pest damage. (And, of course, provides a healthier, mixed diet as well.)

There is another reason why mixed plantings may be less prone to pest attacks, and that is the unhealthy environment created by a single planting system. It's obvious that large fields of single crops can easily attract destructive insects in large numbers, provide them with unlimited food, and thus create a virtual army of pests.

But there has long been a feeling among people in agriculture that growing too much of one thing has additional negative effects as well. For instance, disease spreads easier. There's nothing to stop it—once one plant gets sick, the disease just spreads down those endless rows. There are no other kinds of plants to act as a barrier against its spread.

Monoculture is just not a healthy way to grow plants. And, as all gardeners know, insects don't pick out healthy plants to feast on.

Just the opposite. Like the great, predatory cats that once roamed Africa, crop-eating insects strike at the sick, the weak. And plantation farming encourages ill health and weakness in its plants:

> If we are now to answer the question, "Has the adoption of mono-culture systems led directly to an increase in the number or severity of pests and diseases?" the answer would have to be yes.
>
> We could add that there seems to be evidence that much of this is due to the uniform and crowded conditions that plantations provide and that the cultural operations associated with these crops have often accentuated problems. (Gibson and Jones, 1976)

Planting Resistant Varieties

"Many of today's popular crop varieties have been bred only to improve yields or processing characteristics, with little regard for their susceptibility to insect feeding," reported researchers at the workshop in Tanzania. "As a result, the 'super yielders' often turn out to be 'super delicious' to both disease and . . . crop pests."

So let's stop feeding the pests! Obviously, the native famine plants we mentioned earlier are naturally resistant to the local pests because they grew up together, so to speak. Most serious pest problems occur when foreigners are involved—either a foreign plant with no inborn protection falls prey to local pests, or a native plant is suddenly attacked by imported pests (like our experience with the Gypsy moth and Mexican bean beetle) for which no local predators exist. So simply going back to traditional ways and growing more native plants in the mixed garden system will do much to minimize losses to insects.

In addition, there are well over 100 plant varieties known that are extremely resistant to the pests that normally pose a problem for that kind of plant. They just aren't chosen in most development schemes. Instead, the experts prefer to plant varieties whose harvest provides fruit or vegetables with consistent shape and ripening time to allow mechanical picking, or of such regular (and therefore, unnatural) dimensions that they all fit into preformed packing crates.

It's time for a change. Instead of choosing varieties whose fruit all fits in standardized boxes, let's grow the plants that repel pests naturally. In East Africa, many varieties of sorghum have been found to be naturally resistant to the sorghum shootfly. Some varieties of cowpea—a very important food crop in the tropics—have been shown to be resistant to green pea aphids and leafhoppers. One African research establishment has been very successful in developing varieties of cotton that repel cotton jassids. And in Tanzania itself, as the workshop we keep referring to (and that the Rodale Institute was very much a part of) was getting underway, researchers were discovering that some local bean varieties seemed to be resistant to foliar beetles and beanflies.

Anti-Insect Cultivation Techniques

Factors as simple as the timing of planting and harvesting or removing spent stalks from the field immediately after harvest have been shown to have a dramatic effect on insect populations.

Obviously, this kind of knowledge can be very valuable to the Third World farmer, and we need to devote more of our energies to educaton about timing and less to insecticide use.

Botanical Insecticides

As we mentioned in a previous chapter, one of the leguminous trees that has so much potential to help African farmers has an additional benefit. The fruit of the neem tree is a very effective natural insecticide. Like most other leguminous trees, the neem has many other uses as well, but its natural insecticide production makes it a unique addition to the mixed garden system.

Possibly the best known plant-based insecticide is pyrethrum. Although it has as chemical-sounding a name as some of its more ecologically destructive artificial cousins, it is really nothing more than crushed-up chrysanthemum petals. However, this natural, plant-based product is an extremely effective insecticide that, after doing its job, quickly becomes inert and decomposes—like any other plant material—back into the soil.

That means it doesn't make birds extinct or disturb the local ecology. (You do, however, have to be careful not to kill predator insects when you use it.) And—best of all—insects don't seem to be able to develop resistance to it. (Perhaps that's because it's a natural, and not a chemical product.)

And the world's second largest producer of this natural insecticide happens to be Tanzania! So we know that it can be produced in Africa, in bulk. Raising the chrysanthemums that provide pyrethrum, in fact, could be an excellent cash crop enterprise. And employing people to package the finished product would be a wonderful way to help the local economy develop in a productive, nondestructive, but industrially progressive manner.

Biological Controls

There are two main aspects to the integrated pest management (IPM) technique: the cultivation and release of beneficial insects to prey on pests and the release of sterile insects to interfere with the breeding of pests.

As I write this chapter, the state of California is once again in an uproar over the return of the medfly (short for the Mediterranean fruit fly). California feels that this imported pest is an enormous threat to its fruit crops. The uproar comes because the chosen response to the appearance of this tiny little fly is to saturate massive portions of the state with the highly toxic insecticide malathion via aerial sprayings. Residential neighborhoods are being soaked with the poison (which, of course, authorities claim "is not at all dangerous to human health").

And why is California—the state that otherwise certainly seems to be in the forefront of antichemical enterprise and legislation—being drenched? All because there is a shortage of sterile male fruit flies to release instead, report the newspapers. Those sterile males, released at the right time, in the right spot (especially if aided by the use of pheromones—chemical scents that would attract fertile females to the areas where the sterile males were released), could possibly end the infestation, or, at the very least, begin the process of population control that would eventually do so.

But no. Instead, helicopters drench neighborhoods with chemicals. Parents clutch their children in fear. Windows slam shut. The streets are as empty as in the wake of a nuclear attack. The sound of helicopters in the night is now a serious source of stress. All because, somewhere along the line, those sterile males got slighted while chemicals were stockpiled and helicopters were kept at the ready.

A lot of money changes hands when millions of gallons of pesticide are purchased every time a fruit fly is spotted in California. The successful release of sterile males might just end that flow of cash. And cash does talk.

It just struck me that if the natural pest control methods we've been proposing for Africa were actually adopted, we'd be treating the people in the Third World better than we now treat ourselves. Although nothing would make me happier than to see beneficial insects replace pesticides right here in the U.S., too. Imagine! No more gallon jars of toxic chemicals on sale in supermarkets and hardware stores. Instead, massive shipments of lacewings, lady-bugs, praying mantises, Trichogrammas, and other beneficials ar-riving daily.

Which would you rather do? Put on gloves, long pants, a long-sleeved shirt, goggles, and a mask and go out to spray poison on your tomatoes? Or nail a tiny little paper cup filled with wasps that almost look like dots onto a nearby tree and then, weeks later, note that the only caterpillars in your garden are shriveled, dead husks?

My editor, Mike McGrath, once visited a beneficial insect "fac-tory" not far from Los Angeles for *Organic Gardening* magazine, and he assures me that it is a business that could employ millions nationwide.

He saw endless rows of boxcars where gypsy moths were raised. That's right—the notorious pest of eastern forests lovingly reared like a family pet—by the millions! Because the eggs of this destruc-tive moth turn out to be a favored food for the billions of Tricho-gramma wasps that are produced by this facility every year. Moth eggs are collected, adult wasps are turned loose to do what come naturally, and the facility then ships the parasitized eggs out to gar-deners and farmers around the country. Instead of a caterpillar, wasps emerge from the eggs, anxious to repeat this cycle of cater-pillar control in your garden or on your farm.

The same basic technique holds true for ladybugs, mantises, lacewings, and sterile insects as well. You raise them, ship them, and then sit back and let nature go to work. Research studies al-ready report over 120 different pests being partially to completely controlled by beneficial insects.

It's our choice—if we are willing to accept the responsibility to help motivate such a change, that is. Frankly, I feel that beneficial insects are a lot easier to use than chemicals, and obviously, they pose no threat to the environment. Released in large enough num-bers nationwide, Trichogrammas might well decimate the gypsy moth as a side effect of their garden protection. But the chemical lobby is strong and determined. It will take much courage and determination to force them to face the harm they cause.

Pesticides *breed* bugs. But when farmers see more bugs, they use more pesticides. Those pesticides breed more bugs by fostering resistance and by destroying natural predators. The farmer sees all these bugs, and buys even more pesticides. The cycle has to stop somewhere.

Save the Third World, but don't ignore America either. Even if agricultural chemicals were somehow found to be safe for people who eat the food grown with their use—and I believe very strongly that these chemicals are anything but safe—there would still be good reason to phase them out.

Have you ever seen one of the factories that makes these poisons? Almost always, these chemical plants tend to be located near large bodies of water, mostly rivers. Mostly rivers that supply drinking water to millions of people.

Watch the stuff that pours out of the waste pipes of these factories and into those rivers. Watch for an hour. Multiply that hour by the hours in a day, the days in a week, the weeks in a year, and the years since World War II when this production of poisons went into full swing.

Now multiply that hideous amount of pollution by the enormous number of factories working away at it.

It's a chilling thought.

We don't want to put anyone out of work. But we would like to see a lot of people change jobs. There *are* other jobs. Would it really be that much of a sacrifice to leave behind an eight-hour day of exposure to cancer-causing chemicals and get involved in something a bit more constructive? Like raising and distributing beneficial insects.

Don't want to work with bugs? That's fine. Millions of workers will soon be needed to rebuild this country—in many places from the ground up. I don't want to get too far off the famine track, but the Rodale Institute has also spent a lot of time and money on plans to regenerate America's cities. I don't think anyone out there disagrees that there's a lot of work to do in that regard.

America's cities are a problem that won't go away. And experts agree that it would be a powerful boost to our economy to employ Americans to rehabiliate those cities.

Take the long view. Assume that we have the intelligence to make the changes that will help *us* avoid Third World-style famines in the future. No lost jobs. New ones instead. Construction, not destruction.

But industry, by its very nature, is not going to change willingly. Rather than address the harm that's being done—both by its products and its methods of production—the pesticide industry will spend its energy lobbying politicians and spreading bald lies to the people in order to gain support. I'd rather try to have some drinkable water around in the next ten years.

And it's worse on the farm. The chemical factories that manufacture the pesticides aren't the only point of pollution. In addition to the waste products they contribute to our waterways during manufacture, the finished products themselves pose a threat to our water supply. According to a growing body of evidence, pollution from chemical use on the farm may well be a bigger threat to our supply of clean water than the stuff those big pipes keep pumping out. There's growing concern over the number of wells in agricultural areas that are becoming seriously contaminated by pesticide and chemical fertilizer runoff.

One of our magazines, *The New Farm,* did an undercover survey a while back. Posing as farmers, our staff contacted public and private test labs and asked them how much chemical fertilizer they were supposed to use. The answers varied wildly. Some of the usage rates that were recommended were double and triple the amount necessary.

When you put too much fertilizer on a field, excess nitrogen winds up in the nearest water. That could be a lake. Or a pond. Or a well. Maybe your well—certainly *somebody's* well!

You may already realize that many of the chemicals that have been banned in the U.S. are actively sold in the Third World. You may have seen the horrifying images of children swimming and playing in chemical pesticide drums filled with water. Or families using the drums to actually store precious drinking water. It doesn't take a lot of thought to realize that, in countries where illiteracy is the norm, written instructions and safety cautions aren't going to be read, much less understood, much less followed. Pesticide poisoning is already a terrible problem in the Third World.

And then there is the pollution of water supplies by chemical runoff. The Third World is already short on water. Using chemicals that pollute the little water the people *do* have seems like a supremely foolish recommendation to their farmers.

How's this for a slogan to bring the hard-to-convert into our program: "Don't do it because it's right; do it for the money!" Many economists agree that North America's future virtually requires that the people of the Third World eventually become consumers of our products. But if we firmly entrench the idea that all we offer is death and deprivation, that's just not going to happen. Let's aim a little higher than the unnecessary baby formula, cigarettes, and pesticides that seem to be our favored exports to these proud, wonderful people. They deserve better. Let's take the long view.

You don't even have to do it because it's morally right. You can do it because it also makes economic sense.

Simple solutions work best. Frankly, I don't think we'll ever need giant facilities to breed beneficial insects in the Third World. Most of the great insect predators are native to the tropics. All we have to do is stop killing them with insecticide and encourage their presence with mixed plantings. Those same mixed plantings will also discourage destructive insects. Resistant species and repellant plants will also help.

Again, no roads will be necessary to truck anything in (so it can be stolen by warring factions). No ground water will suffer. No children or farmers will be sickened.

Only the bugs will suffer. And isn't that supposed to be the point?

CHAPTER EIGHT

In the Sudan or Seattle, Humus Is the Hope of Us All

I could write a whole book on humus. Moist and black and full of life, humus is the crumbly, rich-in-organic-matter component of soil that makes farmland come alive.

Humus looks good. If I showed you a field whose soil was rich and black with humus and then showed you a field of the same size that relied instead on chemical fertilizers, you'd probably point to the field full of humus and say, "That looks like great land."

And you'd be right.

But most of U.S. agriculture gave up on humus years ago. Humus comes from natural things. It is alive because its components were recently alive. Manure. Plant material. Rotting leaves. Once living things that—as they decompose—cradle and cultivate other living things such as earthworms, nematodes, and thousands of varieties of microscopic beneficial organisms.

But this rich black earth has been rejected in favor of chemicals by the bag, box, sack, and drum full. A natural cycle that had been uninterrupted for millions of years—plants growing in dark, rich soil, living out their lives, dying and decomposing to become part of that dark, rich soil—was suddenly changed with the advent of chemicals.

Dirt was out. What was in? Powdered, granulated, and liquid nitrogen and nutrients obtained from toxic sources combined in a mixture so overwhelmingly strong it could grow crops planted in just about anything. And those chemicals did their job well for a number of years. Sure, they poisoned the water, and often the people who worked the land, but they *did* grow crops.

All the while, however, billions of acres of topsoil were being lost. Washed away by the rain, blown away by the wind. Normally, that soil would be replaced with humus—with manure and compost simply moved from one part of the farm to another. But not any more. This was farming by the bag and the drum—not farming that relied on deep, rich soil.

Gradually, more chemicals were needed to grow the same amount of food on the land as the soil kept slipping away with no replacement. But those chemicals add no bulk, no living matter to the earth. And, of course, this is the system of farming that we've sent to save the Third World—where the soils are much less rich to begin with. It's a wonder that they've survived our help this long.

Without humus, there can be no food. Famine reigns. Sooner or later, we simply must turn our attention toward rebuilding the world's soil. Expert after expert has gone on record to say that the move away from natural farming, from the simple building up and protection of fertile topsoil, is having a devastating effect on the Third World. For example,

> Chemical fertilizers, even if affordable, are not sufficient and can even be harmful, especially in the sandy soils found so extensively in the Sahel.

In these soils, organic matter is the key to fertility; without it fertilizers are largely ineffective. Ways must be found to manage the total biomass—crops, trees, bushes—so as to feed the soil as well as people and their livestock.

The techniques of environmental regeneration, land regeneration, in Africa are, by and large, the same techniques used to intensify food production. (Peter H. Freeman, consulting geographer, testifying in 1985 before the U.S. House Subcommittee on Natural Resources, Agricultural Research, and Environment.)

Freeman described himself to the House subcommittee as having a master's degree in tropical agriculture and forestry. He had (at that time) worked for twenty-two years in developing countries. For the past ten years, that work had been in Africa, specifically in the Sahel.

Freeman had a lot to say about the special problems of growing food in areas where the climate is often severe, to say the least. He pointed out that, in his experience, the big government organizations were very poorly organized and accomplished little. Rural village groups, however, he found to be well organized.

In terms of workable solutions, he told the committee, he recommends windbreaks to prevent soil erosion and increase crop production. He also likes water harvesting—a method of collecting, saving, and using whatever rain does fall. And he told the committee that he is especially impressed by the potential of one specific leguminous tree, an acacia, that drops its leaves during the rainy season, literally fertilizing the crops underneath with no human help whatsoever.

But his principal message to the lawmakers was about the soil. The land. The earth itself. Unless we take care of the land, he told the members of the committee, "we cannot have stable or sustainable agricultural production in Africa."

How can we have come so far from our basic roots as people who have eaten the fruits of the earth for centuries that such a thing now needs to be said?

By the time I was twelve years old, my father and our whole family had become deeply involved in organic farming. Both the physical realities of the work and the philosophies behind the movement became a part of my basic nature. There are two intellectual roots to the organic method. One, popularized by Rudolf Steiner in Germany, is rather mystical. I never liked it much, and neither did my father. The other is the English root, going back to Sir Albert Howard. His way was based on wisdom gained through observation of the earth and primitive peoples. Howard's work was the inspiration for much of what our first publication, *Organic Gardening*, came to support.

Now, as we apply Howard's organic philosophy to the situation in Africa, we bring his work full cycle. You see, it was by observing farmers in a developing nation that Howard first formed his theories. He had been sent to a village in India under orders from his British superiors to eliminate the primitive methods of agriculture being practiced by the natives. But he saw that what those natives were doing was actually working pretty well. So, instead of eliminating their system, he decided to just try to improve the way they did things a bit. (Which is, you'll note, the very same approach that we feel must be adopted by modern experts and developers if we are ever to attain the goal of long-term food security for the people of Africa and other Third World areas.)

From the time I was twelve, I knew that my life's work would be to take the ideas, the strengths, and the logic of the primitive agriculture practiced by native cultures and try to get American agriculture to be more like that. In the pages of *Organic Gardening* magazine, we took the basic methods by which native peoples around the world were working in harmony with nature, tried to find ways to make those ideas better, and then encouraged people to grow that way.

For almost fifty years we did this. We took the best part of native agriculture, massaged it, enhanced it, made it better where we could, and left it alone when we couldn't. Now we've come full circle. We're taking those methods back to where we found them. And we're saying, "We know that the experts have tried to sell you on a lot of chemicals and artificial ways of doing things, but it turns out that your old ways were better. So here they are again, and this time we promise not to try to talk you out of using them.

"You may think that the streets are paved with gold in America, and that any idea or product from that fabled land of opportunity *has* to be superior. But, while we *are* a wealthy country, we are a wealthy country that has come to relearn the value of manure."

Life is a series of cycles and circles. We in the organic gardening-farming field learned most of our natural growing techniques from the knowledge passed down by generations of native peoples farming in harmony with nature. We took what we learned and— fighting hard against the massive chemical industry and its powerful lobby—have kept alive the idea that you can grow all the food you need without poisoning everything in sight.

Finally, it seems that our patience, perseverance, and persistence is being rewarded. Our old ideas are slowly gaining a new level of acceptance. As the dangers of chemical farming become more and more apparent, the notion of growing food naturally has once again entered the mainstream. Organic gardening and chemical-free farming are not just for kooks and crackpots any more.

The National Academy of Sciences now agrees that sound natural agricultural practices work just as well as chemicals. They also agree that the organic method costs less, doesn't poison wells and workers, and doesn't pollute our lakes and streams.

We've known this for fifty years, of course. But now scientific studies have finally gotten the experts to concede that we have been right. That scientific backing is very necessary to people of a certain mind-set. Now that we have it, there is one less roadblock to taking this knowledge back to the people we learned it from and saying, "Here is your old wisdom. Some of us were saving it for you while others were trying to sell you things.

"Now that we know that those new things don't work, here are your old ways back. They can feed you. They can save your family from famine.

"Feed the soil—as you once used to—and the soil will feed you in return."

First published by the Oxford University Press in 1940, Howard's book *An Agricultural Testament* was unavailable for years before Rodale Press picked up the rights in the 1970s. We've kept it in print ever since.

That book is the seed from which *Organic Gardening* sprouted and the root of my love for the living soil that is humus. I recommend the book highly. It is both a timeless and a visionary work. Chemical farming techniques were still in their infancy when Sir Albert wrote, "The purpose of this book is to draw attention to the destruction of the earth's capital—the soil . . . and to suggest methods by which the lost fertility can be restored and maintained." And the following words—the very first words that appear in the book—should be carved in stone in every farm field and be a requirement of any agricultural project anywhere: "The maintenance of the fertility of the soil is the first condition of any permanent system of agriculture."

Howard calls Nature (which he always capitalized, and in speaking of him, so shall I) "the supreme farmer" and laments that "little or no consideration is paid in the literature to the means by which Nature manages land.

"Nevertheless, these natural methods of soil management must form the basis of all our studies of soil fertility."

Howard asks the question, "What are the main principles underlying Nature's agriculture?" His answers give us a new appreciation of the intricacies of environmental interaction:

Mixed farming is the rule. There is never any attempt at monoculture [in Nature]; mixed crops and mixed farming are the rule. The soil is always protected from the direct action of sun, rain and wind. In this care of the soil strict economy is the watchword; nothing is lost.

The whole of the energy of sunlight is made use of by the foliage of the forest canopy and of the undergrowth. The leaves also break up the rainfall into fine spray so that it can more easily be dealt with by the litter of plant and animal remains which provide the last line of defense of the precious soil.

These methods of protection, so effective in dealing with sun and rain, also reduce the power of the strongest winds to a gentle air current.

The rainfall in particular is carefully conserved. The fine spray created by the foliage is transformed by the protective ground litter into thin films of water which move slowly downward, first into the humus layer, and then into the soil and subsoil. . . made porous. . . by a network of drainage and aeration channels made by earthworms.

There is ample humus for the direct absorption of moisture. There is remarkably little run-off [and] when this occurs, it is practically clear water. Hardly any soil is removed. Nothing in the nature of soil erosion occurs.

There is therefore little or no drought in forest areas because so much of the rainfall is retained exactly where it is needed. There is no waste anywhere.

The forest manures itself. It makes its own humus and supplies itself with minerals. If we watch a piece of woodland, we find that a gentle accumulation of mixed vegetable and animal residues is constantly taking place on the ground and that these wastes are being converted by fungi and bacteria into humus.

They are sanitary. There is no nuisance of any kind—no smell, no flies, no dustbins, no incinerators, no artificial sewage system, no water-borne diseases, no town councils and no rates.

The mineral matter needed by the trees and the undergrowth is obtained from the subsoil. This is collected . . . by the deeper roots. Even in soils markedly deficient in phosphorus trees have no difficulty in obtaining ample supplies of this element.

No mineral deficiencies of any kind occur. The supply of all the manure needed is automatic. . . . Humus provides the organic manure; the soil the mineral matter.

The soil always carries a large fertility reserve. There is no hand-to-mouth existence about Nature's farming.

The crops and livestock look after themselves. Nature has never found it necessary to design the equivalent of the spraying machine and the poison spray for the control of . . . pests [or] vaccines and serums for the protection of the livestock.

It is true that all kinds of diseases are to be found here and there among the plants and animals of the forest, but these never assume large proportions.

The principle followed is that the plants and animals can very well protect themselves even when such things as parasites are to be found in their midst.

I hadn't really noticed it before I sat down to reread his book, but Howard's summing up of the reasons why we should pay closer attention to that most successful of all growers, Nature, reads very much like our plan for famine prevention:

Mother earth . . . always raises mixed crops; great pains are taken to preserve the soil and to prevent erosion; the mixed vegetable and animal wastes are converted into humus; there is no waste; the process of growth and the process of decay balance one another; ample provision is made to maintain large reserves of fertility; the greatest care is taken to store the rainfall.

In other words: Mixed crops. Erosion prevention. Getting that manure and foliage out of the fire and back into the soil. Using everything at hand. Water harvesting.

Sir Albert just about said it all.

So why is Nature denied? Sir Albert also noted that "although half a million examples of the connection between a fertile soil and a healthy plant exist in India alone . . . modern agricultural science takes no notice." Why? Sir Albert felt that it was "largely because they [the natural systems] lack the support furnished by higher mathematics." In other words, statistics. Chemical farming had them; natural farming did not.

You'd think that the successful operation of actual farms by actual farmers under actual conditions would be the best support of all. Unfortunately, to science then—and to science today—that's not the case. In fact, the basic situation has not changed much in the fifty years since Sir Albert wrote those words. Science still loves numbers—Howard's "higher mathematics"—and still has little more than disdain for the actual experience of farmers.

As we said before, the researchers in charge of spending vast amounts of money on foreign aid programs are often more interested in the results they achieve in some laboratory or using some theoretical computer model than in what occurs—what has proven itself over centuries—in the actual fields they hope to grow food in.

That basic disregard for reality has been a sore point with me for many years; a blind side that has worked against the scientific arm of agriculture since Howard's time (actually, since long before).

Most scientists and researchers have always been loath to work with farmers and are brutally slow to accept suggestions, revisions, improvements, advice—even basic facts—from the people who do the growing. The result has been the adoption and spread of methods of farming that move further and further away from Nature's ideal system. Ignoring all the free fertilizer—the raw material that's already there for the taking. Choosing instead to truck in artificially created chemical nutrients.

"These are better," they say. "Look at these numbers on the bag; you know exactly what you're getting." And so for years, Nature's own fertilizers have had to take a back seat to chemicals in a bag. Chemicals that, it now turns out, have wreaked havoc with our water supplies.

But more importantly, their use has robbed the user of massive amounts of the principal ingredient necessary for our species's continued survival—the earth itself. Land across the globe, once excellent growing soil, is gone—eroded away as a result of modern farming practices. And not just in the Third World, either. America has lost much of its once-rich soil.

Where has all that soil gone? It's been washed away to clog rivers, streams, and, of course, those million-dollar dams, on its way to the sea, where it is lost to us forever. In 1984 the Worldwatch Institute estimated that 24 billion tons of soil were being lost from the world's croplands every year. That equals the loss of the first 18 centimeters (about seven inches) of soil on 23 billion acres of land. *Each year.*

But you don't need to lose all 18 centimeters to see a disastrous effect. Research has shown that losing just 1 centimeter of topsoil reduces wheat yields by as much as 50 pounds an acre, reduces corn harvests by as much as 115 pounds an acre.

Some erosion will occur in any farming system, of course. But modern chemical farming is especially brutal in this regard. Chemical farming uses huge amounts of herbicides to ensure its goal of completely "clean" agriculture. No other plants anywhere. That means that, during the growing season, much of the land's soil isn't held down by roots, so it washes away. Between growing seasons—when the land is simply laid bare to the winds and rains—the effects can be devastating.

But the alternative—the organic method—doesn't devastate the area. During the growing season, many noncrop plants are simply left alone. This doesn't cause nearly as many problems as you might think. The plants provide beneficial insects with a place to live and keep the soil in place, protecting the land from erosion. Between seasons, "green manures"—leguminous plants that provide large amounts of nitrogen and other fertilizing elements when plowed under—hold the soil in place and protect the land.

And by using lots of compost, manure, and other natural materials as fertilizer, the organic method doesn't just protect, it actually adds to the soil. After all, what is soil, anyway? The humus portion—the constantly changing, nutritionally alive, topmost element of soil—is decayed trees and branches and leaves and brush. It's dried-out manure and worm casings and other substances created by Nature to provide the earth with everything needed to grow food to sustain us.

But the chemicals created by science to improve on Nature (never a very smart thing to try) add nothing. No dark, rich black earth. Just chemicals. The result is that we—all of us, worldwide—are short on soil. And at risk of famine.

All the solutions we have proposed: a mixed garden system, leguminous trees, the freeing up of manure for the garden, water harvesting—all have a common goal. They create more biomass, more raw plant and animal material to rebuild the soil, to make it fertile again.

Do you realize how ironic it is to have to argue this point? To have to fight with scientists and researchers over the benefits of fertile soil in agriculture? And yet it *is* a fight; make no mistake about it. Many development programs are still built on techniques of soil destruction, not enhancement.

In their 1989 report suggesting that a wonderful plant known as vetiver grass could be a great method of controlling soil erosion worldwide, the National Academy of Sciences (NAS) and the National Research Council (NRC) point out that

> Often the very practices that cause erosion in the long run lead to short-term production gains that create an illusion of progress. Yet erosion is slowly eating away the economic security of dozens of countries.
>
> This is a vital and universal problem, not only because less soil means less food and forestry, but because most of the world's poor depend on the thinnest and most fragile soils for their standard of living—and even survival.
>
> Failure to respond to the erosion threat will lead not only to the degradation of the land, but to the degradation of life itself.

One reason why science has failed to respond is that erosion isn't showy or flashy. It's a slow deterioration. To stop it would require that people take action without a visible and obvious disaster on hand. As the NAS-NRC report explains,

> Erosion is a quiet crisis, a human-made disaster that is unfolding gradually. The soil washes away in small yearly increments instead of dramatically all-at-once.
>
> And the erosion problem will not disappear. Indeed it seems certain to get worse. Future expansion of crop production in developing countries will of necessity have to rely on . . . the farming of nonirrigated lands, many of them on slopes.
>
> Therefore, the threat of soil loss and destruction will rise.

That, in a nutshell, is why we have written this book. If famine is to be controlled in the Third World and if we are to avoid its clutches ourselves, we must rededicate all our agricultural practices to rebuilding the land.

The issue is really so simple that you can judge the merits of any agricultural technique by the answer to just one question: Does this technique add organic matter to the soil—or at least help to retain the soil that is already there? Chemicals do not. Tractors do not. Plantation farming systems do not. Alley cropping, mixed gardens, native plants, and water harvesting do. And so does vetiver grass, by the way.

I'm glad the authors of the NAS-NRC report on vetiver grass were so eloquent about the necessity of protecting the world's soil. Because, in coming back to their comments on the need to build humus in the Third World, I was reminded that I had to find a place to mention the tough little plant they propose as a partial solution to the soil problem.

Study after study has shown that vetiver grows best where erosion's threat is the worst. Vetiver grass is a "low-cost way to protect billions of dollars of investment already made in agriculture, forestry and public works throughout Africa, Asia, and Latin America," says the NAS-NRC. "Major improvements in environmental management and economic development in Africa, Asia and Latin America could result." Vetiver's benefits are so impressive and its applications so diverse, the NAS-NRC report adds, that the grass could become an environmental safety net built into almost all future projects as well.

That's a wonderful phrase: "an environmental safety net." Wonderful, and a physically appropriate image as well. Because this grass *is* a safety net, a safety net for soil. Planted in strips, vetiver grass acts very much like a net as it catches soil and prevents it from washing or blowing away. As the NAS-NRC report explains,

The stiff lower stems act as a filter, allowing excess water to drain while barring the movement of sediments and soil. Equally important, the dense, narrow bands of grass slow down runoff so well that much of the rainfall can soak into the soil before it gets a chance to trickle down the slopes.

This added moisture allows [nearby] crops to flourish while unprotected neighboring ones are lost to [lack of moisture].

We know the system works. Plantings made in Fiji in the 1950s are still stablizing slopes after more than thirty years. In the Caribbean, vetiver plantings are still doing their job after fifty years. And in Africa itself, vetiver has been keeping the soil in place on some erosion-prone slopes for more than sixty years. It is not a temporary solution.

A one-time planting of the grass can supply the same benefits as techniques that otherwise require days of back-breaking labor. This would free up African women and reduce their burden considerably. As the NAS-NRC report explains,

> For the last 60 years, conventional methods [of erosion control] have relied mainly on physically changing the contours of the land to reduce slopes and impede soil loss. These engineered contours are costly and difficult to organize, construct and maintain in developing nations.
>
> By contrast, the use of vetiver grass seems inexpensive, easy to understand and implement, and could be quickly adopted by millions of farmers.
>
> Vetiver could prove to be a billion dollar boon to dozens of nations.

There is certainly a place in our famine prevention plan for such a grass. Especially since those are just some of the benefits. Like most of the other solutions we have developed and/or endorsed, vetiver grass has multiple advantages.

One of those advantages is lack of maintenance. Vetiver does not spread. It does not need to be trimmed back. Vetiver only grows upward to form dense, soil-catching hedges. It does not grow outward. And, since it produces sterile seeds, it is not a threat to nearby crops.

Vetiver can even provide a cash crop. The grass is actually cultivated in some areas for its fragrant roots, which produce an oil used in the perfume industry, according to the NAS-NRC report. Those roots aren't something you could actually farm in the kind of system we're describing, but if you ever needed to get the vetiver out of an area, you'd get a nice, marketable crop of roots for your trouble.

The same deep roots that anchor the grass firmly in place can draw up water from much deeper than most plants. Vetiver will therefore survive the worst droughts, which is good, because the rains that follow a drought are the most destructive to the soil. Vetiver will be there to harness those rains and keep the soil where it belongs.

Vetiver grass holds back so much runoff that the entire area around it is watered by its presence. Wherever you plant vetiver grass, moisture levels in the soil improve over a wide range of nearby land. Describing results in Fiji, the NAS-NRC report says, "the vetiver system [provides] far more direct economic benefit than just halting erosion. By improving the moisture levels, vetiver has become the keystone to sustainable production and increased incomes . . . at virtually no cost to the farmer."

Vetiver's crown, the vulnerable portion of the plant, is located below the soil line, making it virtually indestructible. "Neither fire, grazing, nor trampling can destroy it easily," reports the NAS-NRC. (In fact, grazing animals don't like to eat vetiver, which is very good news, because few plants can survive in areas where animals are allowed to graze. Grazing animals are responsible for much erosion and soil loss when they overeat, stripping an area of all its moisture-absorbing plants. But with vetiver around, grazing animals are less likely to turn once-productive land into more desert.)

The plant will grow just about anywhere. The NAS-NRC report states that vetiver grass "grows vigorously in many types of soil . . . and climates. In India, for example, vetiver is found in the rainforests, the deserts, the black-cotton soils and the snows of the Himalayas."

The grass can even survive complete submergence in water, thus helping protect dams, dikes, and canals during floods, and has the potential to make tree-planting programs more successful. Presently, explains the NAS-NRC report, some tree plantings fail because the young seedlings are not well protected during the early stages of growth. "By providing windbreaks, vetiver strips would be particularly valuable in [these] early stages," the authors explain.

Vetiver grass could be of great use in water-harvesting diversion schemes. As we'll explain in detail in an upcoming chapter, much water can be conserved when the path of rain is slowed on eroded hillsides by the use of natural barriers. Strips of vetiver make great natural water barriers. And without such barriers, the massive amounts of water often contained in desert downpours would simply be lost (along with the hillside's soil).

Because it is also acutely aware of the problems that have occurred in the past with single plantings, the NAS-NRC report adds that alternatives to vetiver should also be investigated. Even though vetiver grass certainly seems to be a perfect solution to many famine-related problems, the authors—wisely—say that researchers should still keep their eyes open for other, similar grasses and hedges "should vetiver eventually show unexpected problems in widespread future practice." Such a statement is the final sign of a well-thought-out, quality proposal.

If the developers and experts had been half as cautious with their solutions, there might not have been a need for this book.

All our recommendations—water harvesting, vetiver grass, leguminous trees, native plants—will serve to protect the fragile soils of the Third World. Those solutions will help hold in place the soil that has not yet been washed or blown away. And, by creating more organic matter (the leaves and branches of leguminous trees) and freeing up other sources (such as animal manure), we will slowly reverse the trend that has made so much of the world so vulnerable to famine.

Imagine! *More* soil, not less. Slowly, the poorly used earth of Africa and other Third World nations will begin to change in color. Now a lifeless yellow, tan, or gray, the soil will first move up in color to a medium brown, then to a deeper, richer shade—a vibrant, chestnut brown—finally to become the rich black earth that radiates with life.

Rich with living nutrients, decomposing slowly and naturally. Energetic earthworms, aerating and enriching the soil. Countless micro-organisms of all kinds breaking down plant and animal matter into rich, sweet-smelling earth that contains all the nutrients necessary for healthy plant life.

Can't you just *smell* that earth? The life in it?

You can almost see the desert recoiling in response—its sandy fingers stopped, then pushed back as the earth begins to change in color. Bleached white sand and useless yellow earth evolving slowly but steadily into rich black soil sparkling with the lush green of life-giving vegetation.

Soil, after all, is the bottom line—not just of any successful famine prevention project, but of life itself. Plants are the essential green link in the food chain, and need good earth to grow in. Are we so foolish as a civilization that we actually will risk breaking that chain?

Again, it astounds me that this has to be said—that reasonable people must actually put forth and support the argument that soil quality is an important factor in the growing of food, that the precious soil we've lost over the years should be replaced, that the fields of the earth should be made whole once again.

But we must. As we mentioned before, a massive multibillion-dollar industry has risen up, and its survival is based on people choosing chemicals over soil. Previously—like the marketers who once spent millions trying to convince women that some artificial formula in a bottle was superior to the milk that came naturally from the breast—these self-appointed experts claimed that chemicals were *better.*

More recently, their claims have become less brash. Now the standard selling premise is one of equality—that bags of chemicals are an acceptable *substitute,* an alternative to building up the soil.

Needless to say, the chemical option is one of Famine's favorites. Imagine with me again, Famine in living form, a personification of that most dreaded of the Four Horsemen of the Apocalypse. You can see this image of death and destruction shrink back in horror from the concept of rich, black earth daring to encroach on its sprawling desert—that vast, sandy plain that provides Famine with so many victims.

Or you can see that same skeletal image smiling a terrible grin as it views the barrels being trucked out of the chemical plants, the poisonous liquids being sprayed across the land, the sheen of a toxic coating appearing on the water of a pond, the birds and insects dying.

We have worked for Famine for much too long, in too many ways. For too many years, we have not fought against Famine, but have instead indirectly allied ourselves with this skeletal foe and worked to its advantage. We have made Famine's job an easy one.

No more. It is time to stop the poisons. It is time to stop the spreading of harsh chemicals on degraded land in the hopes of coaxing just one more harvest out of the burned-out earth. It is time to feed the earth, to return the life-giving energy contained in plants and manure back to the land, where it belongs. It is time to once again see Nature as the perfect gardener and stop believing so foolishly that we could somehow—by whipping up poisons and petrochemicals in our test tubes—improve on Nature's work. It is time to feed the earth so that the earth can continue to feed us.

The work of the Rodale Institute and Rodale International has not been limited to researching, developing, and reintroducing native plants such as amaranth and leguminous trees. Quite a bit of our work in Africa lately has been in teaching compost-making techniques in small African villages. In fact, my son Anthony, a photographer at Rodale Press, has visited and worked on such projects.

As with almost all the techniques we recommend, our compost projects simply take an ancient technique back to the people whose ancestors originally developed it. Sometimes there are minor improvements. Sometimes the system was nearly perfect to begin with. In the case of composting, we have recommended the construction of pits so that the compost—a combination of plant litter, animal wastes, and just about any other organic matter that will provide nutrients when it rots—decomposes more quickly without any loss.

We work on developing ways to construct these pits with a minimum of effort and required maintenance, so that the available organic matter can be used with the greatest efficiency. There are a variety of techniques that we use, depending on the needs and climate of a specific village. All the different varieties of the basic technique have one thing in common, however—they provide a rich, black earth from material that might otherwise be wasted or ignored.

And, of course, we encourage planting systems that make use of techniques to protect this soil once it's in place.

Rich organic matter filled with the essence of life itself, humus is soil and fertilizer in one perfect package. It still astounds me that space and words need to be devoted to the promotion of humus. I am almost reduced, I feel, to having to argue that air is good or that we should drink clean water. And yet those two seemingly obvious arguments are also denied every day by industries that foul our air and water in the name of jobs, progress, and—more honestly— money. Maybe it shouldn't surprise me that, in such a society, voices must be raised in the defense of dirt; that the topsoil of the planet needs a spokesperson to defend it.

So let it simply be said that any solutions to the problem of hunger and famine in the Third World must be solutions that add to the soil, that enrich it with natural, organic matter. (But it still makes me sad that it needs to be said.) Since 1940, 5 million hectares— that's more than 12 million acres—of land have been lost to the desert. The future of this planet demands that we take some of that land back. Trees can make strong inroads. Water harvesting can help greatly. Native plants are essential.

But only humus can make it happen.

CHAPTER NINE

Fight Famine and Ease Population Pressures: Break the Chains of the Women of the World

"Women do 90 percent of the work on African farms."

I remember the first time I heard that statistic. I thought, "That sounds like a pretty strong exaggeration. Still, African women probably do more of the work than most people think."

The second time I heard the issue discussed, the 90 percent figure was quoted again. I began to think that women probably did perform at least half the work on African farms.

The next time I heard the 90 percent figure repeated, I told myself the actual figure probably was more than half. Much more.

And then I went to Africa myself.

Women do 90 percent of the work on African farms.

There is a poem, called the "Song of Ocol," by the Ugandan poet Okot p'Bitek, that I came across in Lloyd Timberlake's book *Africa in Crisis* (1985). A few lines from that poem begin to paint the picture:

> Cook . . . baby on your back
> Washer of dishes,
> Planting, weeding, harvesting
> Store-keeper, builder
> Runner of errands.
> Cart, lorry, donkey,
> Woman of Africa
> What are you not?

The answer, unfortunately, is "landowner, student of helpful agricultural techniques, and beneficiary of education." But that is what she must become if the crisis in the Third World is ever going to be reversed. Women are the key to helping the people of the Third World develop agricultural systems that will both feed them and begin the process of regenerating their cruelly misused land. Because it is women who will do the work, they are the ones who must accept and implement these changes. Many people—those who truly understand the situation in Africa (and many other Third World locales)—have said the same thing in the same words so many times that it seems like one giant universal quote ringing in my mind: "Any solutions for Third World farmers must be solutions that work for women."

Because (especially in Africa) those Third World farmers *are* women. Hideously overworked women. Solutions that don't quickly make their life easier are worthless to them and will not be adopted. These women have no more time to waste, no more energy to invest.

Their burden is so large that it causes hunger to occur in families who actually have food to eat. People working for relief agencies have seen it: After caring for the farm, the family, and gathering the day's wood and water, many women are simply too exhausted to prepare the food they have. Every aspect of this book has been written with these women in mind. Their plight is not an issue we have emphasized along the way, but it has guided my thoughts since my first trip to Africa many years ago.

A Ghanaian physician once commented—all too accurately, I fear—that "the rural African woman is the most underprivileged of all human beings." In a very true sense, the goal of this book is to relieve some of the massive burden on the African woman. And the burden is so massive, so almost unimaginably exhausting, that simply relieving the smallest bit of it will be a tremendous achievement in limiting human suffering.

But relieving that burden will have another effect as well. Expert after expert agrees: Making life better for women is a key component to slowing the explosive population growth in the Third World. Yes, family planning is extremely important. And the destruction of family planning services in the Third World that occurred during the Reagan administration must be reversed. But history has shown time and time again that nothing slows explosive population growth with more certainty than economic security and increased opportunities for women.

There are several issues to cover in this chapter. First, we have to look at the reality of the day-to-day life of the African woman. Once we see what she is up against, we can make certain that any solutions we propose or support cause her no new, added burdens, but really do lessen her daily load.

Second, we must explore how we are going to reach her. It is not an easy task. There are cultural restraints against teaching women in general, and it is often impossible in many developing countries for women to own land (or anything else). Still, women can be reached—they must be. We will examine some wonderful success stories that show how to do that.

And third, we will hear experts on the situation in Africa discuss how easing the burden of women naturally results in a lower birthrate.

Why do women farm in Africa, and why is it getting harder to farm? In *Africa in Crisis*, Timberlake explains:

> Men are forced to leave farms to find paid work in cities, work which often cannot be found.
>
> So women must labor on the farm, or go out to work on bigger farms to earn the cash the men are not sending home.
>
> Kenyan researcher Professor Philip Mbithi estimated that even when the man is on the farm, nearly half of his activities are not directly related to farm work.

And, as Timberlake points out, the environmental degradation that Africa has suffered has also greatly increased the workload of African women:

> As trees disappear, fuelwood sources move further from home. Women in northern Ghana may need a whole day to collect three days' supply of fuelwood, often walking eight kilometers with babies on their backs to . . . collect the wood.
>
> Soil erosion may also mean that women have to work more land or land further from home to grow food for the family, and declining water resources means they must walk further to collect water.

Like the degradation of the land, political and social changes that occurred as a result of colonialism also made women's lot worse in Africa. The two biggest enemies of women in this regard, explains Timberlake, were "the introduction of European legal systems and the advent of cash crops." The new European or colonial way of doing things caused much land to be placed under the ownership of men, even if that land had previously been a part of a woman's traditional family holdings. And the money to be made from the newly introduced cash crops especially "encouraged men to take over women's land rights," he adds.

Those cash crops, he notes, are an especially sore point with African women:

> Research around Africa has found that wives nearly universally oppose cash crops because they reduce the amount of land available for food. This would not matter so much if women were given a proportion of cash returns, but such money is usually considered part of male income.

In addition, remnants of the colonial way of doing things ensure that African women "get little help [with their farming] because extension workers and researchers direct all their attention to the men who are officially in charge of the farms." The men may not actually *do* anything on the farms, but they get the advice. Often, there's no choice. In many parts of Africa, there are cultural restraints against women being educated. And if the extension worker is a man, allowing him to speak with the women who actually grow the food is often unthinkable.

In a presentation to the House subcommittee on hunger in Africa back in 1985, Christine Obbo, a sociologist-anthropologist from Wheaton College who has studied African women extensively, explained that this sexist attitude is not part of traditional African culture. Like corn, plantations, explosive population growth, and famine, she agrees that this lack of basic rights for women is yet another legacy of colonialism:

> All available evidence suggests that what "yoked" African women [a reference to a previous speaker who said that African women's problem was that they were "yoked to a traditional culture"] was not traditional culture. . . .

[People] must stop blaming "tradition" and "culture" for which they have little understanding. Instead I suggest they focus on the real causes [of] the oppression of African women.

[This] so-called traditional culture . . . was a creation of Colonial domination which changed people's relationships to each other and how they did things.

Economic demands in the form of colonial taxes added to women's work burden, she notes. And European-style laws took away women's rights to land, money, and education.

A recipe for poverty. And Obbo notes that the goal of smaller families "will be rejected or ignored unless the major reason for large families—poverty—is shown to be . . . controllable."

My good friend Gus Speth, president of the *World Resources Institute,* explained the situation this way at the committee hearings:

Present laws and practices related to land ownership, credit and extension services mostly exclude women from access to loans and education, although women are an essential part of farming and food production in sub-Saharan Africa.

In many African cultures women have traditionally played a major role in trade as well as shared ownership of the land. However, the introduction of European legal systems has encouraged single ownership by men.

Moreover, recent migration by men seeking employment in urban centers has placed even more responsibility on women to sustain their families' food needs, and environmental degradation has further increased their workload.

Denuded landscapes and scarce water supplies mean vast distances must be covered and long hours spent gathering firewood and water.

Going over these thousand pages of hearings, I am impressed by the attitudes and ideas of many who came to testify. While reading one report on "agroforestry" (growing trees and other crops together) I was pleased to see that John Michael Kramer, a renewable natural resources program coordinator for CARE (Cooperative for American Relief Everywhere), simply referred to farmers as "she" or "her" throughout his testimony. I'm glad to see that some people are paying that much attention.

In the section of his report entitled "The Smallholder Farmer: Her Problems," Kramer explains that

It is difficult for western people to understand the depth . . . of the difficulties she must face every day.

Our farmer rises before dawn to start a fire for breakfast—a rough gruel and a glass of tea. She may then send her children or go herself to fetch water from the nearest well (often quite distant).

If she is running low on firewood, she will take a machete or small hand ax and, in the company of a group of neighboring women, set out for a day-long trip to gather dead branches and twigs.

If the fuelwood supply is ample, she may spend the bulk of her day in the garden or the fields tending crops with a homemade hoe. Near dusk she will return to relight the fire and cook a dinner similar to breakfast.

Too often her day is interrupted by the need to care for a sick child and, when severe illness strikes, a long journey to the nearest health clinic.

Because the land she tends is less than she actually needs to grow enough food for her family, she finds that, with time, her crop yields are diminishing. In order to produce enough grain to see her family through to the next harvest, she has reduced the fallow cycle . . . reduced yields follow.

Now she has to use the animal dung that once fertilized the field for fuel because she can't afford to spend the extra time needed to gather enough firewood.

Everyone [in the village] has the same complaints. She could move, but that would mean leaving the home of her grandparents and her relatives; her only social security.

She stays and hopes. If another drought comes she knows she may not survive, but what alternative is there?

CARE's answer to that question is much the same as our own. More trees must be grown to ease the firewood burden. A burden that drains these women of their days and their energy and robs the field of that good manure.

Once again, it seems that the biggest problem in the Third World—especially in Africa—is not the lack of food, but the crucial shortage of wood. In fact, Kramer cites a World Bank statement that the land in the Sahel—one of the most famine-prone regions in Africa—could grow enough crops and support enough livestock to sustain its growing population. But the Bank also states that the need for fuelwood in that same area is seven times greater than the land can sustain. And, unfortunately, Kramer reminds us, those quickly vanishing "trees are the principal means for lands to sustain their fertility." So another vicious cycle is set up.

The need for more trees is crucial. Alley cropping and other tree-growing techniques are the single most certain way to ease the burden of African women.

CARE has some good, workable plans to grow more trees. And some successes to report in this endeavor. "In Africa, where high-capital agriculture has largely failed to meet the needs of the people, agroforestry holds the greatest promise for resolving gaps in the basic needs of the rural poor," states Kramer in his House subcommittee testimony.

Speaking of the woman farmer, he explains that

With the help of an extension agent or a trained farmer-leader, she can learn the properties of the various trees that will grow in her vicinity and identify the products she desires from trees.

Once [the women in] a village [have] gone through this stage, CARE will provide . . . assistance, materials and equipment to start a small tree nursery to produce the desired seedlings.

Typically, a group nursery produces 2,000 to 10,000 seedlings per year to be distributed among the [village] members in exchange for their labor in the nursery.

And CARE is careful not to make the common development mistake of insisting that these trees be planted in plantations or other off-farm sites. Kramer explains,

CARE emphasizes on-farm planting for several reasons. First among these is "tree tenure."

If a farmer plants a tree on her own land, then she feels more certain that she will receive the benefits of that tree. Ownership results in a greater sense of responsibility for tending the tree and the chances of the tree surviving are enhanced.

This is a lesson that well-meaning developers have been slow to learn. Trees planted off the farm, even in supposed community areas, simply never do as well as trees whose owners are more clearly defined. In much of the Third World, there is a great deal of suspicion about getting the benefits from anything not on your own land.

CARE's other reasons for its on-farm tree planting preference are precisely the reasons we mentioned in previous chapters: so that farmers can make use of the natural fertilizing properties of the leguminous trees. So that the roots can help hold fragile garden soils in place. So that leaves and fruit from the trees are readily available to feed people and animals. So that the leaves can be used for mulch without having to be carried long distances. And so that the wood the trees provide is especially handy.

Other benefits cited by CARE are that trees can be used to form windbreaks, property barriers, and contour rows (an alley-cropping technique in which trees catch and hold the soil from hillside erosion and form natural, plantable terraces over time, thus freeing people from the extensive digging and soil rearrangement tasks that terracing usually requires).

And, finally, trees are a valuable source of cash. That cash comes from gum. Gum arabic, to be precise. When extra space is available, CARE notes that farmers traditionally spread the seed of the *Acacia senegal* tree across a barren field. Within five to eight years, the trees that result will give off a very valuable sap whose sale "may account for half of a farmer's yearly income." And it's a reliable yearly income for the next decade, as well. Then, when the sap flow tapers off, the trees are cut and sold for firewood.

Because the land has been fallow for so long (and because the acacia that grew there is a fertilizing leguminous tree, and the leaves and branches have enriched the soil) the soil's growing properties have now been regenerated. As CARE notes, after the cutting, "the fields are ready to farm again for three to five years."

Obviously, the problem with such a system is the up-front wait for that first year's sap. That's why CARE has added a small improvement to this old technique: The farmer is encouraged to plant seedlings instead of seed to cut that time lag to a minimum (and begin to hold soil in place that much earlier).

By working with local organizations and finding farmers who were already interested in using trees to improve their land, CARE has had some good success with such plans. To control the Sahara-bred winds threatening a valley in Niger, where, CARE reports, "quite literally, the desert seems to be on the move, engulfing the countryside," trees were planted (by the natives themselves) as windbreaks.

This is not a new project. It began in 1974 and was reported on in 1985. But it was small, it met the needs of the people, and it involved those people directly in the decision-making process. As a result, CARE reports that "the work parties have the air of a festival."

And so the plan succeeded. The desert is being denied. And the villagers, explains Kramer, "are convinced that the windbreaks are improving their agricultural productivity," as well. This is confirmed by a small Dutch study that found crop production to be increased by an average of 23 percent.

But the biggest success in this venture is that "nearby villages have asked CARE to help them start their own tree planting program." At last report, this program was underway at five new sites. As many knowledgeable people have said, "The African farmer is not slow to adopt techniques that work."

Kramer also reports on an area in Kenya, where the problem is too much rainfall that often washes away fertile soil. CARE began a trees-for-firewood (and, of course, erosion control) program. They had hoped that, over a three-year period, they could create 36 nurseries to produce 1.6 million seedlings. "By the end of the second year's planting season, the project had created 79 nurseries and planted 200,000 seedlings more than expected."

And CARE constantly reaffirms that the secret of these small (but wonderful) successes is that—unlike the typical development experts, they enlist and win the support of the local peoples. That support is something CARE considers to be "far more important than [the] number of trees planted" because it ensures that the plantings will continue long after CARE has left.

Gaining that local support is one strong reason for CARE's success. And the fact that their representative chooses to refer to African farmers as "she" and "her" is another. It's easy for faraway experts to forget that African farmers are women. But CARE, especially in these instances, has not. Those trees will go a long way toward reducing the daily burden of local women.

Claudine Schneider, a member of the U.S. House subcommittee on hunger in Africa, was extremely effective in keeping the issue of women in the forefront during the hearings. Here she points out the tremendous waste if women are not reached in a more substantial manner:

> The United Nations Economic Commission for Africa strongly noted . . . that . . . economic production would be depressed and many important opportunities of African development would be missed if we fail to provide adequate extension services and training for African women.

She also notes that, although

> Somewhere between 60 and 80 percent of all agricultural [product] that is raised throughout the world is produced by women . . . it is tragic to recognize that less than 1 percent of all agricultural land happens to be owned by women.

My good friend Albert Meisel, executive director of the League for International Food Education (which goes by the wonderful acronym LIFE), suggested in later testimony that the home garden system we endorse would help ease this economic imbalance: "Home gardens . . . provide a source of cash income for families. In at least one documented case, they have provided an alternative to villagers [leaving the farm] in search of wage labor." And these gardens can also help prevent the tragedy of families losing everything in a famine. As Meisel notes, the food—and cash—provided by "home gardens can reduce a family's debt to, and dependence on, traders during hard times."

Those traders are the ones who buy (at bargain rates) everything a starving family owns. So that when the famine crisis is over, even if the family has survived, it now has nothing. And that kind of crushing poverty, of course, is one of Famine's favorite friends. A return to home gardens really *can* help break this horrible cycle.

Meisel quickly adds that home gardening can do all this *without* adding to the burden of women. Just the opposite, he explains. LIFE's research found

> That gardening (unlike farming) is not in fact all done by women. . . . One of the beauties of [home gardening] is that it can be done . . . by people who are otherwise not productive and cannot add to the family budget; that is, older people, children, and sometimes even the men, curiously, because they take an interest.

Meisel explains that this help with the growing of extra food "adds to the resources" of African women and makes the family stronger. "And when the family becomes more self-sufficient, the woman becomes more powerful. That is my belief, in any case; and I think that belief is shared by a great many other people." I believe that as well. The challenge is in reaching the African woman and helping her achieve these advances.

As Peter H. Freeman, the geographer, reminded the House subcommittee:

> Women . . . have little power over rural development, although women are the major food producers, fuelwood collectors and users.
>
> Development planning is an urban, male, bureaucratic and technocratic activity [performed] by those who do not depend on the environment for their security.

The result, he explains, is an unending series of short-sighted, short-term projects that leave the land—and its women—in much worse shape than before.

And his reasoning is right on target. A system where men who are far away and who have little idea about the day-to-day work of farming and gardening, are nonetheless making decisions for the women who really have to do the work, is bound to fail.

The solution is obvious. Women must regain their lost status in Africa.

A major topic of discussion during the House subcommittee hearings was the role of family planning and population control in helping to eliminate hunger in the Third World. That's an important issue. As the chairman of the subcommittee hearings pointed out, "Experts predict that 20 years from now, there will be a second Africa, equal in size to the current Africa of about 450 million [people].

"In other words, in two decades . . . sub-Saharan populations will double."

And unbelievably, at the very time of the hearings, many of the committee members were actively involved in a desperate battle to allow legitimate family planning programs to continue in the Third World.

Tragically, as witness after witness recounted, just as nations and their leaders were beginning to accept and support contraceptive use, the Reagan administration slashed funds.

As one witness stated,

Unfortunately, just at a time when population programs should be accelerated, current U.S. policy amounts to a giant leap backward. Last year the U.S. cut off $17 million in funding for the International Planned Parenthood Federation, the largest private organization providing family planning assistance to the developing world.

This year [this was in 1985] the U.S. has cut off $10 million of a grant mandated by Congress to the United Nations Fund for Population Activities, the largest multilateral [nonprivate] provider of family planning assistance to the developing world.

And money wasn't even the biggest problem. Instead of offering women information on a variety of safe and effective contraceptive devices, the Reagan administration wanted legislation that would require family planning experts in the Third World to stick to "natural family planning" techniques—things such as the rhythm method—instead. Obviously, the women of the Third World should have the right to make up their own minds on these kinds of issues. They have the right to be presented with a variety of contraceptive choices and then be allowed to pick the one that works best for them.

But there is also another, more subtle—and extremely effective—method that will help Third World people control their massive birth rate. And that is education and an increase in social status and basic rights for women. Throughout history and across the boundaries of civilizations, nothing has lessened the birthrate with more certainty than an end to the oppression of women. As subcommittee chairman James Scheuer put it during the hearings,

> Literacy [and] education is the best contraceptive, and it is essential for women . . . to accept the fact that there is a different role for [them]. . . .
>
> That means that women must have access to education. They must have access to credit. . . . There has been far too little progress in improving and enhancing the status and role of women, and until we do that, all of your garden production programs in the world won't be able to keep up with the . . . population growth rate. . . .

Steven W. Sinding, Ph.D., director of USAID's Office of Population, told the House subcommittee:

> From my own experience in a number of Asian countries, and more recently in Africa, I have become personally convinced that until alternative roles for women are found they won't be interested in limiting family size.

From Marshall Green, a retired ambassador, speaking for the Population Crisis Committee:

> Traditional African societies offer many cultural reinforcements for large families, and in many countries the virility of African men is still viewed as related to the number of children fathered.
>
> A change in attitudes will only come . . . when male perceptions of women cease to be focused exclusively on childbearing, child rearing and doing menial tasks. Strategies to improve the status of women are critical to this process, and AID [the Agency for International Development] should expand its Women in Development program.
>
> AID should increase its support for innovative, small-scale projects . . . for women in developing countries in cooperation with [local] women's groups.

Small-scale projects. That's the key to helping women. And the key to lowering that staggering birthrate.

The simple truth is that every home garden, every alley-cropping success will allow women more time. More time to learn, more time to grow, more time to demonstrate their abilities and to understand that their value—their worth—in life is not limited to childbearing. And, slowly but naturally, the birthrate will fall.

Make no mistake, women in the Third World must be provided information about and access to safe and reliable contraceptives. Those slashed funds must be replaced. But woman-centered, garden-centered, locally controlled small projects—true development—will make smaller families a natural part of the chosen lifestyle of people who no longer live under famine's shadow.

Perdita Huston, former regional director of the Peace Corps, told the House subcommittee how this can happen, how it already has happened, and how such changes have the potential to make development really live up to its name:

The UN Fund for Women, by providing small seed grants to women's projects, has been extremely successful in demonstrating the impact small investments can make on the economic and social well-being of communities.

The Overseas Education Fund, The Center for Population and Development Activities, Women's World Banking, and many others have proved that investment in training and providing credit to women has tremendous dividends.

People-centered development, particular attention to women's roles and status, coupled with . . . sound environmental, population and development planning—from a long-term perspective—is . . . common sense development.

Perhaps the finest example of how things should be done in the Third World was presented by Elise Fiber-Smith, executive director of OEF International (OEF stands for Overseas Education Fund). Founded by the League of Women Voters over fifty years ago, OEF is now independent of the League, but not of women. In her prepared testimony, Fiber-Smith explained that the OEF is "dedicated to enabling women—particularly low-income women—to improve the quality of life for themselves, their families and their communities." In her remarks to the House subcommittee, she summed up what sounds to me like the perfect plan for success in any Third World area:

We don't go in with a formula, but we work at the local level with low-income women, listening to their needs and designing the kind of training that will increase their capability of either generating income [or] increasing food production.

We are a real hands-on, long-term development group.

OEF is much more than that. It is a model of what development should be. If it had been in charge of the billions that have gone to build huge, worthless dams and fertilizer factories, there might not be a reason for me to be writing these words today. Famine would be on the run.

At that moment, back in 1985, Fiber-Smith's group was working at the local level with national women's organizations in East Africa, West Africa, and other parts of the Third World. She knew that other organizations, as she put it, were "giving lip service to the fact that, yes, women farmers are important." But she also knew that these other organizations only had lip service to offer. They "have not figured out the mechanisms to make [things] happen."

But her group *had*. And she had some conclusions to share. The first proposal concerned USAID and USDA training programs: "There needs to be a much greater, tougher look at . . . designing training to fit African women's special needs. . . . We may even want to target that at least 50 percent of that training ought to be geared to women in Africa." (A very modest proposal, considering that women do much more than 50 percent of the work !)

The second proposal emphasized the need to break through the cultural barriers that make it difficult to reach these women:

> From all our experience in the field, there just are not adequate [teaching and informational services] out there reaching local women farmers. We believe that we should be able . . . to strengthen extension services to reach women.
>
> How do we do that? What we hear and what we see out in Africa [says to us] that there have to be actively recruited female extension agents.
>
> I think . . . that . . . organizations . . . need to give more focus on the ways that lighten women's workloads.

The organizations that she feels (and we at Rodale Institute agree) have the best potential to actually make these changes and reach women at the village level are called PVOs (short for private voluntary organizations):

I think AID needs to be directed to increase its support for long-term PVO development, as PVOs are effective [at reaching] low-income woman farmers. [And] I think that experience has shown that they (the PVOs) [can] do more.

She feels (and again, we agree) that the American people already support the basic concept of giving a greater share of the available resources to small, voluntary groups like the OEF. Now, she says, it's time for the U.S. foreign assistance efforts to look more to them as well.

It is frustrating that her wonderful words were spoken five years ago. Frustrating because so little has changed since then.

The people in charge know about the problems. The people in charge know that raising the status and improving the education of African women will do much to solve the problems facing that continent. And yet, inertia still rules. Big organizations move slowly. They pay lip service and agree in principle, yet resist change until it is forced on them.

In the last chapter of this book, I will call on you to do just that. To take the information that everyone in the business of fighting hunger and famine has known for so long and put pressure on the people in charge to really make use of that knowledge. To that end, I will simply repeat Fiber-Smith's closing remarks to the committee, and hope that now, five years after they were spoken, we can at least begin to change the final portion of those words:

We have a real moment, a real opportunity. Suddenly, it is like the world has awakened to the fact that we have got to do something with women farmers: we have got to reach women in rural areas. But nobody is setting out the strategies and the mechanisms to do it.

The overall strategy is a simple one. As she says in her prepared statement to the House subcommittee, "Long term [development] can only be attained when women have *access to and control over resources and benefits* from their labor." (Her emphasis, by the way.) Moreover, although women are almost always excluded from the decision-making process, "it is clear," says Fiber-Smith, "that women's participation strengthens any development program, anywhere." OEF has many success stories to prove that point; in Morocco, Panama, Honduras, and El Salvador (where, with OEF training, women rose from poverty to form a successful tomato-processing cooperative that in 1985 had 200 members and was profitable enough to secure loans for expansion).

In Africa, the OEF points out, "women are the first to suffer" from the damage done to the land by colonialism and development:

> They need to work harder to get the same harvest. They have to walk long distances as fuelwood becomes more scarce. Wild plants gathered by women, which are important sources of fuel, fiber, fodder and medicine are fast disappearing. Less desirable land and steep hillsides are being cultivated. Yields are falling.

Her solutions? Not U.S.-style farming, that's for sure: "Large equipment, such as tractors, is often uneconomical and sometimes has had negative results overall." She feels that the overall plan for improving the status of women should begin with "a broad range of subsistence crops, agroforestry and . . . simple ways of increasing soil fertility."

And we need more, better trained women extension agents to go in and help African women re-establish what worked so well before. To help women once again make use of "the rich store of indigenous knowledge which has enabled them to survive over the centuries." She notes that "Where women have received [such] agricultural extension services, production has increased significantly."

In the final comments of her prepared statement, Fiber-Smith recounts that she had attended the 1985 Nairobi conference marking the end of the U.N. Decade for Women. It was not, she recalls, a time of celebration:

> Despite overwhelming evidence of the vital role that Third World women play in the development of their countries, we are concerned about policy trends [that place] emphasis on fewer, yet larger [development] programs.
>
> [This] reverses the progress made through smaller model projects aimed at economic development and self-help efforts, as mandated by Congress over 10 years ago.

She refers to the Office of Women in Development, which Congress made an official part of USAID some time ago. It is time, she says, to remind the U.S. Congress of its legal, legislated commitment to Third World women.

If anyone emerges as looking less than sterling in the House subcommittee hearings, it is USAID. And in a way, that's good news. Because that agency controls much of the money that now makes Third World people more vulnerable to famine, but which, properly used, could reverse that vulnerability.

Here's what their representative had to say about a "surprising" success involving women:

> Earlier this month I was in Malawi where I personally saw one of the best water projects that I have ever seen, and probably one of the best in the world . . . providing water to about 100,000 people— clean water.
>
> [US]AID is paying only for supplies. The villagers themselves do the construction. At each of these villages the management of that tap and the management of that water is entrusted to the women. It wasn't the men who managed the water use. Interestingly enough, it was the women who were in charge.

He reminds the committee that, although "very interesting," such a situation unfortunately is also "very atypical."

"The farmer and her husband"—that wonderful phrase comes from Loret Miller Ruppe, the director of the Peace Corps—whose members happen to be some of the most positive influences on people in the Third World. The Peace Corps has always stood for small, local projects that really do help people, as opposed to the big projects that just leave them more vulnerable.

At the time of the hearings, Ruppe remarked that half of the Peace Corps' membership was women, and that half of the total number of Peace Corps volunteers were working in sub-Saharan nations, "involved in agriculture, food production and rural projects . . . helping the small-scale farmers, who are mostly women." She said that the struggle to bring knowledge and income to Third World women was "the challenge of the 1980s."

Obviously, it has now become the challenge of the 1990s. But we cannot ignore the challenge for still another decade. There is simply no time left. Africa's population is already well on the way to doubling itself.

I have no illusions about this massive population problem. Any brakes we apply in the form of elevating the status of women and lessening their workload will be slow brakes. But they will have permanent effects. We simply cannot wait any longer. We must begin to apply those brakes now. In reality, famine is a women's issue. And by helping women, we can defeat famine.

In 1973, the Peace Corps' "Women in Development" mandate came about in response to an amendment to the Foreign Service Act that called for particular attention to be paid to the integration of women into U.S. assistance programs. In 1978, the Peace Corps Act itself was amended to include outreach to women "as an integral part of agency policy." Here's how the actual amendment was written:

In recognition of the fact that women in developing countries play a significant role. . .the Peace Corps shall. . .give particular attention to those programs, projects and activities which tend to integrate women into the national economies of developing countries, thus improving their status and assisting in the total development effort.

Unlike other agencies with similar mandates, the Peace Corps has lived up to this charge, and performed well for women. In the final chapter of this book, I will call on you to work with me in convincing those others to dig out and reread their mandates about women and to follow in the Peace Corps' path.

As we'll point out, it's not only right—it's the law.

CHAPTER TEN

Water Harvesting, Fish Farming, and Salt-Loving Plants: Making Better Use of the Water That's Already There

The single biggest difference between Africa (or at least the most famine-prone regions of that massive continent) and other parts of the world is water. The Africa that is the most vulnerable to famine is also the driest.

The Sahel, the arid sub-Saharan region of Africa, has always been dry. But the problems we've pointed out in previous chapters—loss of tree cover and topsoil, plantation planting, wrong-headed development projects—have all contributed to making this dry land even drier.

What was once a dry land from which wise people were able to obtain everything they needed to survive has become a land so dry and so misused that it can no longer sustain plant life. Especially when the plants in question are water-loving North American crops.

The changes we have proposed will help. Millions of additional trees—an easily attainable goal—will hold soil in place, shade the earth, and bring deep water up closer to the surface. Native plants—more resistant to drought, insects, disease, and fluctuations in rainfall—will also hold soil in place and shade the ground. Together, the two mean more green—a slow but steady pushing back of the desert. And those simple changes will cause more rain to fall.

Experts agree that the spread of the desert has . . . well . . . encouraged the spread of the desert. There really isn't any other way to say it. The more land area composed of desert, the less moisture there is to condense, rise, and form into clouds that eventually produce rain. And, of course, the less rain that falls, the more the desert grows.

That situation must be reversed. And trees, humus, and native plants in a traditional home garden system will do much to halt and then reverse the desert's spread.

But much of Africa will still be dry and will always be considered dry by our standards. The experts' answer to such dryness, of course, has been artificial irrigation—the damming up of rivers and the diversion of lakes to try to move water toward potential croplands. Perhaps no other form of development has been quite so destructive.

As I write these words, I simply can't get an article from the February 1990 *National Geographic* out of my mind. The photos and excellent reporting of "A Soviet Sea Lies Dying" document the hideous side effects of artificial irrigation at its worst.

Many years ago, the article explains, the Soviets set themselves the goal of becoming self-sufficient in cotton production. So they diverted two rivers that originally flowed into a huge lake (actually an inland sea) to irrigate land to grow cotton.

Like most truly horrifying schemes, this one seemed to work well for many years. And then people noticed that, without the rivers to sustain it, the Aral Sea itself was disappearing. But the diversion didn't stop.

Now the Aral is half gone. Already, a body of water one and a half times the size of Lake Erie has disappeared, leaving tragedy, death, and disease. In the area around the lake, throat cancer is epidemic, and the infant mortality rate is the highest in the Soviet Union. The cause? Raging, noxious dust storms of salt and dried minerals from the exposed 11,000 square miles of former seabed, that make desert sandstorms seem friendly by comparison. An estimated forty-three tons of salty grit a year is whipped into the air by harsh winds "to harm the people and the land." Those people, says the *National Geographic* article, "feel salt on their lips and in their eyes all the time."

The dried-out lakebed—littered with the rusting hulks of old ships—looks like a scene from a post-nuclear-war film. The image of ships beached on a sea of sand makes our own Dust Bowl of the 1930s look like a swimming pool. "I doubt there has ever been an environmental problem of this magnitude," says an authority from Western Michigan University quoted in the *National Geographic*. The article simply calls the Aral, once lush and filled with fish, "a new dead sea."

Similar fiascos—albeit on a lesser scale—have been repeated many times in the Third World. You simply cannot divert water without consequences. And water diverters, it seems, never consider those consequences beforehand.

In some cases, all that a massive million- to billion-dollar project accomplishes is exchanging one area of dryness for another. You irrigate one formerly dry spot, but the land the diverted river once fed then goes dry. With lakes, diversion causes shorelines to recede. Often the drop in water levels allows the ocean to come rushing in, making the water salty and poisonous to plants, livestock, and people alike. And silt (from erosion) has a habit of clogging up dams and other big water projects as well, limiting to a few decades the life span of systems that were supposed to last forever.

Those are the typical consequences of big irrigation projects. It's true that in North America some such projects have worked. But, by now, we hope we've pressed home the fact that Africa is not North America.

Actor Richard Dreyfuss, one of the members of the group Africa Tomorrow, who testified at the House hearings, put the water situation in a nutshell when he said that "it is apparently not only Africans we are losing . . . we are also losing Africa itself—[to] the desert."

And he understood that this loss was not the result of a natural progression, but had much to do with the misguided help that had gone before:

> Africa is strewn with the bones of the well-intentioned; the inappropriate projects that . . . failed because of a refusal to take into consideration local needs and local customs; programs that neglected to scout ahead, that forgot to marry into the family, as it were.

He speaks of the harm that U.S. know-how has done to the fragile African soil. By simply doing the same things that are slowly ruining American soils, the tractors literally sterilized the less-resilient African soil, perhaps for hundreds of years.

His group's solution? "Restart [the] ecological cycle and let it run naturally, unhindered by . . . fixes . . . funding, or the need for alien experts." Of such an Africa—repaired of the harm done by development and then simply left alone—Dreyfuss says, "It seems to me that there is nothing wrong with this picture." And, of course, there isn't. The image of an Africa whose ecological cycles have been restarted is a lush and pleasing picture indeed.

And it's a picture that doesn't lack for water. Because, as with the solutions we have proposed for Africa's other imported problems, the scarcity of water is something that the Africans themselves learned how to deal with centuries ago. Native cultures developed techniques that allowed them to make good use of the little water available to them. Techniques that must be rediscovered if the continent isn't to dry up and blow away. If Africa isn't simply to be lost.

"Water harvesting." The words have such a pleasant sound. You can almost imagine water farmers carefully tending to their precious liquid crop. (In fact, isn't that what Luke Skywalker and his family were doing on that dry planet at the beginning of the first *Star Wars* film—farming moisture? The need for such an occupation in the future may be more than simple fiction if we don't get smart now!) But for the present, "water harvesting" refers not to the growing of liquid, but to catching, diverting, and making maximum use of the water that does fall—even in the driest areas. Water harvesting is an ancient science, and a highly effective one.

Dr. Cynthia Irwin-Williams, an executive director of the Desert Research Institute at the University of Nevada, explains the traditionally dry state of much of Africa to the House subcommittee hearings on hunger in Africa:

> The region of Africa immediately south of the Sahara is known as the Sahel, and it forms an arid or semi-arid band across the continent. Characteristically, it receives between 100 to 500 millimeters—that's 4 to 20 inches—of rainfall per year.
>
> Accordingly . . . by nature . . . [it is] an area which is subject to recurrent drought . . . [that] will recur over and over again. [Such drought] is not unique to the midseventies and the mideighties.
>
> The agricultural and pastoral techniques presently in use are generally inefficient and in some areas . . . are actually destructive.

The . . . result has been the rapid desertification . . . of huge areas of the Sahel, amounting to the loss of more than 10 million acres to the desert in the last 40 or 50 years.

She explains that the only workable long-term solution is "a comprehensive program using very simple techniques for making best use of scarce water resources." Water harvesting:

[These techniques] require little or no capital investment, can be employed by untrained people using only hand tools, are sustainable over a long period of time with low maintenance and can be integrated into a wide variety of . . . situations.

Indeed, this simple technology provided the . . . basis for major ancient Biblical civilizations in the Middle East . . . but [has] recently been overshadowed by more elaborate and costly . . . schemes."

In place of those schemes, the Desert Research Institute, working in cooperation with Africa Tomorrow, the University of Arizona, and Clark University in New York, has come up with a plan based on the old ways. Explains Dr. Irwin-Williams,

We believe that the introduction or reintroduction of these simple ideas into selected parts of arid Africa will enable the people there to emerge from the present crisis with important new tools to feed themselves and their families and to achieve an increasing degree of economic self-sufficiency.

In contrast to many of the attempts at assistance . . . over the past decade, we believe that this . . . is both appropriate to the environment and appropriate to the cultures of the people.

Let's continue with Dr. Irwin-Williams' testimony:

Water harvesting may be defined simply as the capture of rainfall which is normally wasted on nonproductive areas such as stony hillsides and its concentration in other areas for [agricultural] purposes.

The basis of water harvesting is the fact that, although rainfall is low and infrequent in arid regions, it does indeed produce a considerable amount of water.

Even one-tenth of an inch [of rain] can produce 1,000 to 2,000 gallons of water per acre if efficiently managed and harvested.

A family of six, with camels, sheep, dogs and a donkey need about 18 cubic meters [a meter is a little more than a yard] of water per year, so a single ten millimeter rainfall [less than half an inch] efficiently harvested . . . could supply a herding family's water needs for a year.

By capturing and concentrating this rainfall, water harvesting can provide the moisture necessary for small- to medium-scale agriculture, for forage enhancement, for stock raising and as a source of [clean drinking] water for people and animals.

And she adds that

The fine grain, loose-type soils which are present in most deserts are ideally suited for water harvesting because they . . . form a smooth crust that promotes runoff of the water for capture.

Millions of hectares can be made more productive than they are today.

Experts agree that water harvesting alone can make large-scale farming possible in extremely dry and unlikely places.

Simple techniques—basically clearing and creating a path for rainwater runoff to go where you need it—can be used to water very large fields with the water caught from the rain that strikes nearby, unproductive desert land.

But water harvesting can bring small successes as well. For example, in the desert a favorite technique is to design little runways that carry rainwater to a single valuable fruit tree. You only need the water that strikes about sixteen square yards to keep such a tree alive in a land where three to ten inches of rain falls in a year. "A wide variety of fruits, such as peaches, apricots, and grapes; nuts including almonds and pistachios; grains and forage crops have been successfully grown based entirely on runoff agricultural techniques," reports Dr. Irwin-Williams.

She adds that the United States, Israel, and Australia are the world leaders in water-harvesting techniques, and that projects based on this ancient system have already found great success in Africa, India, and Central America. And not everyone has had to *re*discover water harvesting, she adds. "In some areas, some surviving preindustrial ethnic groups still use the technique." (That's nice to hear!)

Irwin-Williams told the House subcommittee back in 1985,

We believe that . . . water harvesting technology has the potential for making a substantial impact and for providing at leat a partial solution to the problem of water scarcity in the arid Sahelian region of Africa.

At our own initiative and at our own expense we at the Desert Research Institute at the University of Nevada have already undertaken preliminary studies . . . [of] the Sahel and have determined that acceptable *and even excellent* conditions exist over wide areas.

That's an exciting statement. And what she says afterward gives that statement added credibility:

In order to avoid repeating past errors, any program . . . [must] be truly appropriate to the recipient culture. . . .

This requires an understanding and appreciation of the real economic needs of the people . . . their culture . . . and an identification of culturally acceptable mechanisms for . . . acceptance.

If those conditions can be met, I strongly feel that any strategy designed to help Third World peoples is almost guaranteed to be a success.

And I agree with Dr. Irwin-Williams that the water-harvesting techniques she describes are "appropriate to the environment and to the cultures of the people and can be easily integrated into the solution of a wide range of . . . problems." Here are short descriptions of some of the principal types of water-harvesting techniques, as presented to the subcommittee by Dr. Irwin-Williams:

• *Catchment harvesting.* An area of otherwise unusable land is slightly modified by removing plants, rocks, and gravel and compacting the dirt and sand so that no water is absorbed into the soil. When it rains, the drops strike the earth and roll as if it were concrete. The flow of this runoff is then diverted to crops, pasture, or a storage area (such as a well) by a series of simple ditches and/or rock walls.

• *Water diversion.* Existing gullies that formed naturally over time (and turn into raging streams when rainwater runoff rushes in) are diverted from their present, often destructive, course so that the water instead flows to fields or wells. Basically, this is a variation on catchment harvesting where nature has already provided the catchment area and the first ditch. All the people have to do is divert the water from that ditch toward crops or wells. And when the pathway is also terraced, the flow is slowed down so that greater use can then be made of the water along the path. Erosion is also controlled naturally.

• *Water spreading.* A slightly different use for a natural watershed. Rainfall that usually rushes down gullies to be quickly lost is diverted along the way by a series of small, handmade ditches, dikes, "spreading dams," and living fences of brush that spread the raging water gently onto adjacent areas of crops and pasture land.

• *Microcatchment.* The soil around small plantings located at the lowest points of the land is kept loose and mulched. When it rains, the loose soil greatly increases the amount of water absorbed when the runoff naturally flows down to these low points of land. The mulch keeps the water from evaporating afterward.

• *Contour catchment.* A series of sloping terraces spreads the rainwater that rushes down hillsides onto adjacent strips of soil where crops are growing. The addition of gates at each level ensures that water is equally shared all the way down. This not only grows food on an otherwise unproductive area, but helps keep the soil from being washed down the hillside.

• *Artificial springs.* This approach is a little more labor intensive, but worth the effort. To secure rainwater for drinking and cooking, a pit is excavated along the path of a natural watershed. The ground at the bottom is then compacted tightly so that water cannot drain out. Then a pipe is placed in the center leading out of the pit with a tap on the end. The hole is then filled back up with sand or gravel.

When it rains, the watershed will deliver a torrent that will seep through the sand or gravel and deposit quite a lot of water in the pit. You then have a "spring" ready to deliver water for quite a while after each rain. (The sand or gravel will prevent loss by evaporation.)

When House subcommittee workers asked if these techniques really worked—if Dr. Irwin-Williams had actually ever done anything like what she was describing—she told this story:

> I can describe a personal experience with doing some of this about a month and a half ago . . . in an area of central Nevada which has about four inches of rain a year.
>
> Two women, one of them myself, cleared a very small "pilot" area of about 10 by 10 meters (around 120 square yards) in an afternoon by using garden hoes . . . simply clearing a slope of the gravel that allows the water to seep into the ground. Without that gravel present, the water will run off and can be captured.

We simply planted a collection barrel at the bottom of the slope in the modified area and [another barrel] in an unmodified area . . . and we put in a rain gauge.

The next time it rained, we had a one-tenth of an inch shower which produced no water whatsoever in the [barrel in the] unmodified area. There was no runoff whatsoever.

In the modified area, in the collection barrel, [there were] 25 gallons of water. This gives you an idea of the kind of output [you get] for that kind of minimum input.

Twenty-five gallons from a tenth of an inch of rain! That's a lot of water to get in return for an afternoon's work on the part of two people. And, of course, that barrel will continue to fill every time a little rain falls.

The roots of these simple systems are wonderfully close to home—our home, that is. Water harvesting is an ancient American tradition as well. Explains Dr. Irwin-Williams:

In the Southwestern United States, some of the ancient cultures of the Chacoans (an Indian tribe) maintained a very high level of civilization, perhaps the most advanced, most sophisticated of our native American cultures, entirely on the basis of rainwater harvesting.

As a final seeing-is-believing part of her report, Dr. Irwin-Williams showed wonderful photos to the subcommittee: fruit orchards, barley fields and lush pastures filled with sheep—all made possible by water-harvesting techniques alone—in areas with less than five inches of rain a year.

The water is already there. A surprising amount of water. All we have to do is return to the old ways of catching it.

In an earlier chapter, I mentioned ventriloquist Paul Winchell, probably to the disbelief of many of you out there. He hasn't been active in show business lately, but many will remember him as the "straight man" who threw his voice into a variety of scene-stealing puppets, most notably Jerry Mahoney and Knucklehead Smiff.

But what many people don't realize is that the same man is also known as *Doctor* Paul Winchell the inventor. Dr. Winchell created the very first artificial heart and holds patents on many important medical inventions. Among his many areas of interest and expertise is aquaculture—fish farming. And, although it is not as close to African tradition as the other solutions we have presented, I find his ideas and suggestions interesting enough that I would like to see them tried on a larger scale.

Basically, what he proposes—and has shown can work—is to take the most barren and useless land and the abundant amounts of subsurface water that is too brackish for drinking or agriculture and use them to create huge amounts of delicious, edible protein. Protein that the African people desperately need in their diet.

As Dr. Winchell told the subcommittee,

> The things that make our technology unique are:
> One, where other methods require the use of fresh water, ours can thrive in fresh, saline, alkaline, or even brackish water.
> Two, where other solutions need nutrient-rich soils, ours works exceedingly well in the worst, impermeable clay soils which cannot support conventional agriculture due to the fact that water will not drain. And,
> Three, where many systems require costly commercial fertilizers, ours can be sustained by free animal wastes.
> With these three elements we can provide an inexhaustible chain of food supplying a total nutritional balance which, once begun, will continue in perpetuity. The only requirement is supervision, which can be easily taught to the African people.

As Dr. Winchell explains, science has long known that there are "countless water tables not far below the surface of Africa," many of which are located close to villages and other population centers.

But the water is often too salty or brackish for conventional use, so it has mostly been ignored. Winchell proposes that pits be dug and the clay soil be compacted at the bottom. With the hard, naturally impermeable soils found in much of sub-Saharan Africa, this assures a nearly leakproof pool.

Then, the only technology necessary comes into play—a pump to fill the pond with brackish water from the nearest underground source. Most of this water is located close to the surface, so the pump doesn't need to be powerful. And once the pond is filled, that pump would be freed to fill another pond, and so on. A single pump would fill quite a few ponds in its lifetime.

The pond is fertilized with animal waste. Algae grow. Then fingerlings—baby fish that have been raised in a centralized fish nursery (or provided by the nearest already established pool, as we'll soon explain)—are added.

I might not have mentioned Dr. Winchell's plan were it not for the specific fish that he chose to stock these ponds. Yes, this very special species is a native of Africa called the *tilapia*.

The tilapia is described as a very prolific native African fish. Unlike many other varieties, these fish do not eat their young (or any other fish, for that matter), so they are perfect for a fish-farming system.

They are herbivores—algae eaters who thrive on the primitive plant life that forms on the surface of the pond after you throw in the natural fertilizer. Actually, the inedible portions of the fish themselves also happen to make great fertilizer. (Both my editor and I rely heavily on fish-based fertilizers in our own gardens, and a favorite American Indian technique was to simply plant a chunk of fish with each corn kernel, so that the growing stalk would be fertilized as the fish decomposed.)

In tropical countries, recounts Dr. Winchell, one female tilapia can produce 300 to 500 offspring a month. In a typical system, these tiny fish would then be moved to another pond. There, the females would achieve a respectable three-pound size in about six months, after which they themselves would then be able to reproduce. Males would be twice that size.

As you can see, the process of creating huge numbers of fish is so rapid that the originating nurseries might soon be unnecessary, and villages would have a nice cash crop selling fingerlings to start pools in adjacent villages.

Using such a system, Dr. Winchell estimates that each acre's worth of fish ponds would provide seven tons of fish a year. That's a lot of fish. And the leftovers, as we said, make excellent, high-quality natural fertilizer.

And this is not just a theory. As Dr. Winchell told the House subcommittee, he has farmed these fish himself. He has seen this success with his own eyes:

> I worked with these creatures, and I had these ponds. And the thing I'd like to stress is that this is low-intensive technology. It doesn't require anything more than just the ponds . . . the water and the fertilization, and from then on, the cycle just continues indefinitely.

When challenged that the system sounded a little too technological to qualify as a sustainable and simple solution, Dr. Winchell explained,

> Aquaculture goes back to the ancient Egyptians who practiced it 4,000 years ago [when there was no] intensive technological help and knowledge. They were doing it extremely well . . . on a primitive level.

How can you argue with a plan that uses barren land and undrinkable water to create tons of fish that could save millions from a terrible, lingering death?

Especially when the people are already accustomed to eating the fish in question, and little or no maintenance is required to keep production at a massive level. With aquaculture, you're producing food and fertilizer without soil, using solar power almost exclusively.

Some crops actually *prefer* brackish water. Seaweed comes to mind instantly as an example of good food that thrives in salt water. But not all such food grows *under* the sea. Many land-based crops can grow in the harsh, brackish pools of water created by ill-fated development projects.

Africa Tomorrow identifies several food-producing plants that thrive in salt water and are native to Africa—including duck weed, water sprouts, water clover, and water buds. "These plants," they explain, "are rich in carbohydrates and when sun-dried, provide a flour from which conventional bread, cakes and other dishes can be baked." (By now, you've probably figured out that we are extremely impressed by the intelligent, thoughtful, respectful, and ecologically sound solutions proposed by the diverse and talented members of Africa Tomorrow. Subcommittee member Tim Valentine called them "gifted Americans" and "national treasures," adding "I am proud to be in your company." We can only agree, and we are pleased that we can share their creative insight with you.)

During another of the House subcommittee hearings, luck provided a last-minute speaker (he had just forty-eight hours notice) who greatly added to our knowledge of brackish-water crops. Dr. James Aaronson, a professor of botany and an expert in desert farming from Ben-Gurion University of the Negev (the Negev is a desert, by the way) in Israel, just happened to be in the area.

Lucky for us, because he then had the opportunity to share with the subcommittee what Israel—which *must* farm the Negev if its people are to survive—has learned about plants that aren't picky about their water. Israel, he explains, is already using "virtually 100 percent of our available fresh water," and yet has to expand its agriculture into the dry Negev. As in Africa, water is available, but it is not good water.

So, he explains, "farmers, aided by researchers, have learned how to use underground brackish water." Their success in this area, he notes, "has led to the establishment of six new settlements entirely based on brackish water irrigation." Some of the plants they are using are *so* hardy, he adds, that they are exploring "the possibility of using undiluted seawater in agriculture."

The secret of this success? A "different view," one that

> Looks to wild plants that are naturally adapted to arid and saline conditions.
>
> No conventional crop known will tolerate such highly saline water, but we have determined that there are at least 1,750 species of plants around the world that *would* tolerate this type of water.

And it's a good thing there are that many. Dr. Aaronson points out that somewhere between 980 million and 2½ billion acres of land in arid and semiarid regions are currently affected by salt. "Salinity," he explains, quoting from the published agricultural research, "is unquestionably the most important problem of irrigated agriculture."

In India, says Aaronson, 6 million hectares (out of a national total of only 40 million) of irrigated farmland "have been made useless by salinity and waterlogging."

The problem is critical in the Mediterranean, where the cause is clearly due to human activities. "Massive inputs in the form of artificial irrigation . . . tend to lead to salt build-up in cultivated fields, resulting in . . . abandonment of the land," reports Aaronson.

Even California is hard hit. Thanks to artificial irrigation schemes, a million acres of land had been "made useless to agriculture" by 1963! And each year the United States loses an additional 170 to 250 thousand acres "due to salt build-up."

The solution? A family of plants known as the *halophytes*. "Over 32,000 kilometers (more than 65,000 miles) of desert coasts and equally huge areas of sand dunes could be brought under cultivation with the right halophytes," says Dr. Aaronson.

There are more than 1,250 known species of these hardy plants, belonging to at least 100 different families. Already, we know that many can produce a high-quality animal fodder from otherwise unusable land.

But animals aren't the only ones who can benefit from the planting of halophytes. Mangrove trees may be the best known of this salt-loving breed. And they may be yet another way of helping to ease Africa's desperate shortage of wood. These magnificent trees are "an abundant source of timber, firewood and charcoal"—materials which Dr. Aaronson agrees are needed even more than food in much of the Third World: "I believe it is a mistake to focus our entire attention on the problem of food," he told the subcommittee. "We need to think in terms of agricultural systems that can supply sustainable supplies of food, fuelwood and fodder if we want to approach any long-term solutions." And, in Africa, these hardy sources of much-needed wood, like so many of our other solutions, only need to be reintroduced. Part of that once-lush land, explains Dr. Aaronson, contained "formerly dense mangrove forests [that] have been eliminated or greatly reduced."

Other valuable salt-loving halophytes identified by Israeli researchers and reported to the House subcommittee by Dr. Aaronson include:

• *Saltbrushes.* "Important worldwide for forage and fodder," these plants have been researched and cultivated for at least a century. At least one family of saltbrush shrubs is known "to not only survive but also produce exceptionally large quantities of [high-nutrition animal fodder] under extremely saline conditions."

• *Sugar beets.* "The natural salt tolerance of the wild [ancestor] has mostly been bred out of the commercial varieties." However, a little work with some wild varieties should be able to produce a nicely salt-resistant variety of this major food crop.

• *Eelgrass and saltgrass.* Eelgrass was harvested by the Seri, a North American Indian tribe, who toasted and ground its seeds to make gruel. Palmer's saltgrass provides a grain, similar to wheat, from which the Cocopa Indians made bread (they harvested thousands of acres of the grain from the tidal flats of the Colorado Delta). This ancient seed, once thought lost, was recently rediscovered.

• *Date palms.* While not technically considered true halophytes, these valuable trees are felt to have been domesticated from wild halophyte cousins. The date palm's genetic salt resistance is so strong that even today's highly cultivated varieties "can be irrigated with moderately brackish water without serious loss of yield."

• *Rushes.* These water plants have been used since biblical times to make mats, baskets, and rope. Certain species are so salt tolerant that they survive in the Dead Sea's salt water.

• *Sea fennel.* You'll find the young leaves and shoots of this saltwater plant in your salad if you stop for lunch while traveling in Italy or Greece.

• *Halophyte trees.* The Salvadora varieties provide edible fruits, which are rich in oil and fat. These multipurpose trees also provide good-quality wood and animal fodder.

As Dr. Aaronson has explained, several halophytes are known to provide animal fodder of exceptional quality from otherwise unusable water sources. But they generally serve another purpose as well. While providing huge amounts of fodder, a halophyte exper-

iment in a very salty area northeast of Mexico City is also successfully stabilizing the dried-out land.

Much food for cattle is being produced, but experts feel that the
major benefit from the project is the reduction in dust storms that
used to sweep into Mexico City during the dry season. The importance of plant roots keeping soil and sand in place simply cannot be
overestimated.

In addition, Dr. Aaronson explains that halophytes can be used
to landscape areas where the water quality just won't support conventional plants. Growers in America have already picked up on
this, and are using halophytes to protect and perk up salty,
brackish-water areas—especially in Florida.

Perhaps the most important potential use for halophytes in Africa, however, is as yet another source of fuelwood. An almost perfect example is one we mentioned previously—the desert-loving
Prosopis turns out to be a halophyte as well as a legume. Dr. Aaronson cites Prosopis for its high-quality wood and edible seed pods.

Edible oils are a possibility that has not yet been fully investigated, but Dr. Aaronson points out that preliminary studies indi-
cate that the oil produced from the seeds of halophytes may be of
better nutritional quality than conventional cooking oil. That's
certainly something to look into, at the very least.

And finally, Dr. Aaronson suggests that halophytes can serve us
in yet another manner. Research into the secret of their success in
salty water may teach us how to make our conventional crops more
salt resistant as well. And that could well be the most important
contribution of all. For unless we change the way we treat the water
and the land in North America, we'll need that knowledge to avoid
famines of our own.

So you see, Africa isn't really as dry as it seems. The African
people get (or have) all the water they need. They just need to be encouraged to go back to the traditional ways they used to collect and

protect it. And where the water is too salty and brackish for any-thing else, let's plant some halophytes and see what happens. One thing I've learned in researching this book is that if you look hard enough, you'll find a plant that can survive almost any kind of con-dition—while providing something useful to the people who live nearby.

Fish farming? I don't know. I certainly love the idea, and I'd like to see if the natives really would adopt such a concept. Many experts feel that fish ponds do fit nicely into the mixed garden system. I hope that's true. The people need the food.

These are all simple long-term solutions with one thing in com-mon: They wring life-giving water out of a moisture-stingy envi-ronment. And, in doing so, they help save the land and feed the people as well.

Part Three

A Call to Action

CHAPTER ELEVEN

How You Can Save Three Lives

It all comes down to a simple choice—are you for or against famine?

Famine's friends are quiet. They make no noise; they raise no voices. Famine's friends quietly support the status quo. And if you look very carefully you can catch a glimpse of a shadowy figure behind them. Smiling.

Famine's foes are loud. Famine's foes make waves. They make food an election issue. They demand that the world's forests and greenery be protected at all costs. They press hard for change. The shadowy figure behind them is *not* smiling.

As many knowledgeable individuals quoted in previous chapters have explained, hunger is subtle; famine is nigh invisible. It sneaks up on you. It is a gradual decline that often goes unnoticed until the trap has been sprung.

But we can shine a light on the darkness and force famine out in the open before its evil work is done. Remember, "all that is necessary for evil to triumph is for good men (and, I would add, good women) to do nothing."

Let's do something. I figure it will cost you $100. Why $100? Because, despite inflation and the great changes we've seen in the prices of the goods we purchase over the past few decades, that's still the psychological point at which a purchase becomes serious. You can buy something for $75 and not think too long before you write the check. But when you add that third digit, something changes. Suddenly an emotional commitment is required. Simply put, $100 is still the point at which something becomes a lot of money. It also happens to be a substantial enough amount so that your contribution really *can* save lives.

But don't worry if you can't afford to actually give money. Contributing to an organization committed to the principles of famine prevention is just one way to spend your $100. That $100 is just a dollar value; your contribution doesn't have to be cash—$100 worth of your time can save three lives just as well.

The reestablishment of home gardening in Africa and other Third World areas pretty much encompasses all our solutions. By definition, home gardens include a wide variety of mixed plantings. Traditionally, those plantings include a large portion of native plants and trees. And with most of the developing world still dependent on rain-fed (as opposed to artificially irrigated) agriculture, water-harvesting techniques should also be a part of home garden design. The incorporation of trees and the emphasis on natural, nonchemical growing and pest control techniques also ensure that soil building will be a part of any successful home garden plan.

Such a return to an ancient system of survival would do much to prevent famine. Home gardens by the very nature of their mixed plantings discourage insect damage. The use of leguminous tree cuttings from the gardens keeps weeds down and prevents the devastation caused by random cutting of firewood. Home gardens provide a bountiful supply of food, yet are small and unobtrusive enough to escape the notice of soldiers. They require no roads or political cooperation, and are an essential first step in reclaiming land lost to the desert.

We have quoted quite a bit from the House subcommittee hearings on hunger and sustainable agriculture that were held back in 1985. In the final report on those hearings, which was released in 1987, home gardens are shown to be relatively affordable as well. "Funding on the order of $2 million to $3 million is needed to enable private voluntary organizations and the Peace Corps to introduce household gardening in Africa," says the report. (Again, I would have said "reintroduce." Even the subcommittee acknowledges "the fact that in many areas there is a strong tradition of household gardening.")

Only $2 to $3 million. What a small price to pay to deny the desert, to frustrate famine! If I have done my job well enough, if my editor helps me present my words and thoughts correctly, if my publisher, Sierra Club Books, gets this work into enough hands, we can surely achieve that goal ourselves. That's right—we. Us. You and I. The famine fighters.

All we need are 20,000 to 30,000 people to join with us, take this challenge seriously and set in motion the steps that will turn the world into a truly safer place. Safe from famine and chronic, persistent hunger.

In baseball, when you're just learning the game, it's enough to make contact when you're up to bat. As long as you hit the ball, you did well. You didn't strike out.

Giving to charities is much the same. The first couple of times people decide to donate money to a charitable cause are like those first couple of times at the plate. You're not really sure what you're doing, so you just swing away. You really don't think too much about where that ball is going. So you write a check and send it off.

Maybe to CARE, or Live Aid, UNICEF, or Save the Children. You don't specify what you want in return—you don't tell them what to do with that money. You just send it.

And that's a good start. You put the ball into play and there's a chance that good things will happen as a result.

But now I want to take you to the next level. A good ballplayer doesn't just make contact. He or she tries to hit the ball to a very specific area, to a visible gap. Instead of just hoping for the best, you can use your knowledge and experience to try and make the ball fall in a specific place. If your contribution is going to be money (as opposed to, or in addition to time) I want you to place your donation carefully.

If you already have a favorite charity, I want you to write them a letter. Ask three things:

1. Request a brief listing of specific projects that the organization currently supports that are in tune with our famine prevention program.

2. Ask what percentage of money contributed to the organization goes toward long-term, sustainable, small-scale development projects.

3. Ask if you can specifically target a donation so that all the money you contribute (or raise, if you want to save several hundred lives) goes toward sustainable agriculture projects.

If there is a specific amount that you intend to donate or raise, by all means mention it. If it's $100, for instance, that psychological dividing line comes into play again. A $100 donation makes an organization sit up and take notice.

Naming that amount might make the difference between your receiving a form letter and a personal reply. And don't be shy about mentioning that you will pass the word on to others if you do receive a favorable reply.

Here's a sample letter:

Director of Donor Services
CARE, Inc.
660 1st Ave.
New York, NY 10016

Dear Friends:

I have come to believe that the only way to truly combat hunger and famine in developing nations is through long-term sustainable development projects that are small in scale, cooperate fully with native peoples, and protect and improve the environment. I would like to know what specific projects of this type that your organization has recently funded.

Some examples are the restoration of home gardening systems; the distribution and planting of leguminous trees to control erosion and ease the firewood problem; advice and assistance in local composting programs to improve soil quality; small-scale water-harvesting projects; and other programs that have the potential to significantly ease the burden of Third World women.

I would also like to know what percentage of the total funds that your organization receives goes toward such small-scale, sustainable agricultural projects.

And, finally, I would like to know how I may target a contribution to your organization with the assurance that my entire contribution will go toward long-term, ecologically sound projects that are consistent with the goals of *famine prevention*. [If there is a specific figure that you are willing to contribute, mention it here. If you have friends who are also willing to donate if they can receive such assurances, mention them—by name if at all possible.]

I realize that most of your fundraising is probably done through impersonal means such as direct mail campaigns and public service ads, but I urge you to respond to my inquiry.

It is my intention to make a donation toward these goals. However, I will only make that donation to an organization committed to the principles of preventing famine through long-term, small-scale, village-oriented projects.

I look forward to hearing from you.
[Signed] _____

Of course, you can word your own letter any way you want. Try to keep it short. A page is perfect. Anything longer than two pages might not be read. You don't have to type your message, but I can tell you from my years of experience reading the letters that our subscribers have sent in to *Prevention* and *Organic Gardening* that half of the handwritten letters I've seen are unreadable. So if you don't type, print. Clearly.

If you don't already have a favorite charity (or if that charity fails to respond to your letter or sends you a reply that you don't like), try making several copies of your letter and sending one each to several charities. Then you can contribute to the organization whose response is most in tune with the solutions you feel have the strongest potential to end famine. That's right—*you!* Please don't limit your thoughts to what we've said in the preceding chapters. It's important that you think about the issues involved and truly believe in the solutions you choose to support.

If you do decide to send your letter to several groups, you will accomplish several things. You will—by the very nature and wording of your letter—make people in those organizations more aware. Aware that Americans are now willing to take a more active role in solving the problems that cause world hunger than just writing a check. That these Americans are now demanding significant changes in how hunger is fought.

Serving notice of this new level of involvement is a very powerful message to such organizations. And as Amnesty International has shown, the writing of letters is a powerful tool that can have tremendous influence.

Under the guidance and direction of Amnesty, simple letters—nothing more than a few words on paper—have forced some pretty powerful and scary characters to actually release political prisoners from their jails. Imagine! Dictators releasing their political adversaries from prison because a group of individuals in another country organized and wrote letters demanding that they do so! If letters can persuade dictators to release people from prison, imagine the impact they will have on an organization already committed to helping people, but perhaps just lacking a bit in its direction.

Personal letters make a very strong impression—even on large organizations. Let's say that the first thousand people who read this book decide to step right up to the plate. Let's say they knock a letter out straight to CARE, for example, asking them what CARE is doing to prevent famine, how much of its resources are going toward that goal, and if they can direct an entire contribution so that it goes only toward sustainable projects.

A thousand well-written intelligent letters from willing and potential donors will make an enormous impression, believe me. The people in charge will sit up and take notice. They'll ask themselves, "Well, what are we doing that meets the Rodale plan criteria for famine prevention? Are we doing enough of it? Do we have some sort of special fund that meets these requirements? Should we create one?"

I would be surprised if a thousand letters didn't lead to the creation of a special fund earmarked for famine prevention projects. Who knows? Your letter might be the one that pushes the people in charge into making the decision to pay special attention to long-term, sustainable solutions.

A thousand such letters might prompt an organization to launch a new TV, radio, and print campaign to raise funds specifically for famine prevention. Slowly, long-term solutions could become the popular alternative to shortsighted relief and wrongheaded, destructive development schemes.

Whether you realize it or not, these things are all within your power. Your involvement, your willingness to commit yourself and what is, in truth, a very small amount of money compared to what it can achieve, give you power beyond your wildest dreams.

One of my major goals in writing this book is to help make those kinds of waves. To move things to the next level; throwing a spotlight on the way we attack famine and hunger, making it an issue. If I am successful, I believe it will be a true breakthrough.

No one has done this before. Of course, hunger has been an issue for quite a while now. Over the last few decades, people have really become much more aware of the problem and have shown that they are willing to help do something about it.

But the experts and researchers who have proposed the most ecologically sound and workable solutions to the problems of world hunger have never taken their case to the people and asked them to lobby for those solutions. Unfortunately, those with whom we are in greatest agreement—the experts whose solutions have the greatest potential for long-lasting positive change—tend to express their views only in those "shelf" books we spoke of earlier. The information that is necessary for people like you to be able to fine-tune your response to the crisis of famine in the world today has been hidden. It's been shut away in difficult-to-read articles in obscure journals and buried in jargon in books that are never seen outside the confines of a university library.

I hope that this small effort on my part can change that situation. But I am only the batting instructor in this game. In truth, I am not a player at all, but a coach, trying to help you play the game to the best of your ability.

Make no mistake—it is *your* game. *You* are the one up to bat. *You* are the one with the power to cause sweeping positive changes in organizations and attitudes—changes that can save many lives and end much suffering. Changes that can remove much of the pain, frustration, and vulnerability from the lives of people around the world. These wonderful people deserve better than short lives filled with fear and hardship.

If you had asked me what the chances were of such a thing happening twenty years ago, I would have said, "One in 100." (There has never been a time when I would have said that there was no chance at all. Too many things that have happened in this world and in my own life have shown me that nothing is impossible.)

Then George Harrison staged the concert for Bangladesh. That event changed things considerably, breaking through old barriers and bringing to a whole new generation awareness of famine and the need to do something about world hunger. The odds improved greatly. At that point, I would have said that the odds for something like our Rodale famine prevention plan becoming a popular, accepted concept had reached about one in 20.

When Bob Geldof's LiveAid event exploded into the public consciousness, our odds got even better. Almost overnight, more North Americans than ever became aware that massive numbers of people in the world simply did not have enough to eat. And an enormous number of previously uninvolved people accepted some financial responsibility for changing that situation. I'd say that as a result, the odds for success in achieving what we're proposing in this book improved to about one in three.

And now? Now that we've taken that next big step of daring to actually look at and evaluate potential solutions for their strengths and weaknesses, I'd say that our chances have never been better: 50/50. One to 1. Even odds.

For the first time in the many years that I've been involved in trying to help solve the problems of world hunger in my own small way, I can honestly say that I really believe that we can do this. The issue of how we attack hunger and famine in the Third World can become a popular topic. In the past few decades we have progressed, after all, from a nation of people who really didn't recognize the problem, to a nation that did, to a nation that has given massive amounts of money in an attempt to change things. A wonderful progression in a relatively short period of time. A positive metamorphosis.

All we need to do now is to take that final step. We should no longer be satisfied with just writing a check, with sending money to someone somewhere and assuming that our donation will do more good than harm.

I hope I've done my part in illustrating a few of the ways in which that money can be spent most advantageously—ways that help ensure good long-term results without damaging the earth's fragile environment even further. Now it's time for you to use that information. Step up to the plate, look at a few pitches and then place your hit. Yours may well be the letter—the one that convinces the director of a major aid organization to look closely at the Rodale famine prevention plan and make positive changes. *Someone's* letter is going to do that. I would like it to be yours.

Go ahead. Knock one out of the park!

Even if you've never donated a cent to any charity in your entire life, you already give money to an organization that funds projects designed to combat hunger in the Third World. And you contribute on a regular, yearly basis. Or else you're reading this in jail.

That's right—I'm talking about taxes. Just because much of the aid the U.S. government has given in the past has made people in developing nations more vulnerable to famine doesn't mean that we can't change things now. In fact, considering the enormous impact that U.S. programs have on Third World people, we *must* change the prevailing attitude about how that money is spent or all the good work being done by private organizations could go to waste.

I know what you're thinking: What could be more tiresome

than to be told to write your Congressional representatives. How unoriginal. Can't I come up with something better?

No. I can't. Elected officials pay attention to letters from the people they represent. And, again, the way that foreign assistance and development funds have been spent has been a nonissue—up till now.

In fact, about the only pressure on elected representatives in this area so far has come from people who make a profit from the status quo. From lobbyists who want to keep sending massive amounts of animal feed and chemicals to the Third World. Lobbyists who want the government to keep paying U.S. farmers to grow too much, and then to sell that excess to the government or private agencies so that yet another fortune can be made shipping it to unfortunate recipients overseas.

There has been little public call—and certainly no outcry—for the government to switch its emphasis to small-scale, prevention-oriented approaches to the problem of world hunger and famine.

And, again, only you can achieve this change. You don't have $100 to contribute? Fine.

Then $100 worth of your time will do just fine.

You can begin by contacting your own elected representatives. Your state has two senators, both of whom represent you. Your state also has members in the U.S. House of Representatives; the exact number is based on the population of your state. Your personal representative serves your specific geographic area.

If you don't know the names of those who represent you, contact the League of Women Voters in your area. They're listed in the phone book. You can also call or write Washington for the information. The basic phone number you need to know is (202) 224-3121. That is the Capitol building switchboard, and the people at the other end can tell you who your representatives are, and even connect you directly to their offices.

To write to your representatives, address your letters this way:

The Honorable _____   The Honorable _____
U.S. Senate   U.S. House of Representatives
Washington, DC 20510   Washington, DC 20515

But don't stop there. Although you have the strongest influence with your own elected representatives, you should still think of this as a national (actually, a global) issue. You should ask your representatives (or members of their staff, who more likely will be available to speak with you directly) what committees are handling these issues and to whom it makes the most sense to speak or write.

In addition, I am pleased to say that the people who ran the 1985 House Subcommittee on Natural Resources, Agriculture Research, and Environment hearings we have referred to so frequently are still "on Capitol Hill" (at least as of this writing). Their work on the House subcommittee was exemplary, and they are the most obvious central resources and spokespeople for pushing the concept of sustainable agriculture as an international famine prevention policy. They will be the most knowledgeable about what needs to be done to get things moving on this issue once again. Contact them:

• James H. Scheuer (New York), Chairman (then and now) of the House Subcommittee on Natural Resources, Agriculture Research, and Environment, of the Committee on Science, Space, and Technology:

> *Address:* H2-388 House Office Building, Annex 2,
>   Washington, DC, 20515-6303
> *Phone:* (202) 226-6980

• Tim Valentine (North Carolina) and Claudine Schneider (Rhode Island). Both were extremely outspoken on and supportive of small-scale projects, the role of women, and many other basic famine prevention goals during the 1985 hearings.

• Other members of the 1985 House subcommittee who still serve are

Henry J. Nowak (New York)	David E. Price (North Carolina)
John S. Tanner (Tennessee)	David E. Skaggs (Colorado)
George E. Brown, Jr. (California)	Sid Morrison (Washington)
Howard Wolpe (Michigan)	Christopher Shays (Connecticut)
Dave McCurdy (Oklahoma)	Paul B. Henry (Michigan)
C. Thomas McMillen (Maryland)	Lamar S. Smith (Texas)

Your efforts will be doubly effective if the person you contact is a representative of your state. Urge your friends to contact their state representatives as well, especially if those representatives serve on committees or subcommittees that deal directly with foreign aid, farming, and/or world hunger issues.

• The chairperson of the House Select Committee on Hunger is currently Tony P. Hall, a Democrat from Ohio:

Address: The Honorable Tony P. Hall
2162 Rayburn House Office Building
Washington, DC 20515
Phone: (202) 225-6465

• The chairperson of the Committee on Foreign Affairs is Dante B. Fascell, a Democrat from Florida:

Address: The Honorable Dante B. Fascell
2170 Rayburn House Office Building

Washington, DC 20515
Phone: (202) 225-5021

• Then there's the House Regional Subcommittee on Africa. It influences the kind of aid programs that are proposed, and is charged with reviewing the legislation that has an effect on this famine-prone continent:

Address: Regional Subcommittee on Africa
816 House Office Building, Annex 1
Washington, DC 20515
Phone: (202) 226-7807

Now, what do we tell these committees and individuals to do? As with the charitable organizations we mentioned earlier, an intelligent, personal one-page letter can have a tremendous effect.

Around the time of the House Subcommittee 1985 hearings, a number of excellent pieces of legislation were introduced and passed by both the House and the Senate. However, these laws died or fell into limbo afterward and were never sent to President Reagan, who would probably have vetoed them anyway.

But George Bush just might sign those pieces of legislation. When I was at the White House recently, I congratulated the president on his renewed commitment to the Peace Corps, a group identified by almost everyone at the subcommittee hearings as the United States's finest ambassador and the group most likely to succeed when it comes to getting small-scale, ecologically sound sustainable agriculture projects going in the Third World.

During the writing of this book, President Bush set in motion steps to pump up the Peace Corps budget to the tune of an additional $16 million for fiscal year 1991. (That would give the Peace Corps a total of $181 million.) That would be the biggest single jump the Peace Corps has seen in its budget in the last twenty-five years, and it should fund an additional 1,000 volunteers by 1992.

That's good news in a number of ways. First, it's good because the Peace Corps has always led the way in small-scale helpful projects that really work in the Third World. Putting a thousand more volunteers out there has the potential to really give famine a poke in the eye.

Second, the boost is good because the Peace Corps currently has twice as many applicants as it can train and deploy in developing nations. I'd like to see every one of those potential volunteers have the opportunity to get out there and fight famine (and by all accounts greatly enrich their own lives as well.)

But in a much broader sense, this increase in funding is good because it implies that our current chief executive might be willing to do more. Perhaps he might even sign one of the many fine famine prevention bills that made the rounds back around 1985.

Here's a brief rundown on some of those bills that said the right things ("H.R." refers to a bill introduced in the House of Representatives; "S." to one introduced in the Senate):

• *H.R. 2958 (introduced July 10, 1985).* This bill's emphasis is on "biodiversity." It essentially concentrates on funding to preserve native species and a wide variety of the world's plant life. Also an excellent bill.

• *S. 701 (introduced March 10, 1987).* Amends the Foreign Assistance Act to authorize the president

> To provide . . . assistance for long-term development in sub-Saharan Africa.
>
> Requires the purpose of such assistance to be to help the poor majority in sub-Saharan Africa to participate in a process of long-term development through economic growth that is equitable, participatory, environmentally sustainable and self-reliant.

This bill pretty much has it all. It takes the role of women into special account, repeatedly specifies that most funds be spent on small-scale projects in which local villagers are involved from the start, urges that private organizations with a history of success in these areas be the ones who get the money, and strongly urges USAID to get its act together.

• H.R. 2782 (introduced June 18, 1985). Also sought to amend the Foreign Assistance Act to authorize the president to place more emphasis on small-scale projects. Listed are just about every solution we proposed in Part Two of this book: soil conservation, agroforestry, small-scale farms and home gardens, use of organic and regenerative methods, and so on. Here's a sample of the fine language contained in this bill:

> There is substantial and growing evidence that the most effective, quickest and least-costly way of maintaining and restoring the resource base is through small-scale, affordable, resource-conserving, low-risk, local projects, using appropriate technologies and methods suited to the local environment and traditional agricultural methods in Africa, and featuring close consultation with and involvment of local people at all stages of project design and implementation.

• S. 1364 (introduced in the Senate June 26, 1985). Virtually identical to H.R. 2782, this bill is even called "a bill to authorize assistance for famine prevention in Africa." The point of both these bills is to add a new section, called "Prevention of Famine in Africa," to the Foreign Assistance Act.

Believe it or not, this is only a partial list of such bills. There was a flurry of excellent legislation proposed around that time—motivated, of course, by the immediacy of the last big famine. None of the bills mentioned here went all the way, but none were actually defeated, either. In fact, most were passed by both the House and the Senate and then just disappeared in committees (which is not at all uncommon).

That means that any of these bills can be easily reintroduced, polished, and sent to the president. He's the real power here. If you read the exact language of the Foreign Assistance Act as it stands and of the proposed changes, everything refers to "authorizing the president" to do this or spend that. The president is the one who actually administers the Foreign Assistance Act, under which the United States provides almost all its aid to foreign nations.

This act is a complex document. Under it, much of what we want is already law! The Foreign Assistance Act already specifies that the president must support sustainable development, protection of the world's forests, and special efforts to involve women in all development efforts. Here are some excerpts and summaries:

[Section 117 says,] It is . . . in the economic and security interests of the United States to provide leadership both in thoroughly reassessing policies relating to natural resources and the environment and in cooperating extensively with developing countries in order to achieve environmentally sound development.

The President is authorized to furnish assistance . . . for developing and strengthening the capacity of developing countries to protect and manage their environmental and natural resources.

Special efforts shall be made to maintain and where possible to restore the land, vegetation, water, wildlife and other resources upon which depend economic growth and human wellbeing, especially of the poor.

Section 118 states that special efforts be made to protect and restore the world's forests, and adds special provisions for preserving the tropical rain forests.

Section 113, which became law in 1973, specifies that special efforts must be made to involve women in all programs funded under the Foreign Assistance Act. Specifically, it says that those sections that cover funds spent on agriculture, rural development, and nutrition; population planning and health; education; and development projects "shall be administered so as to give particular attention to those programs, projects and activities which tend to integrate women into the national economies of foreign countries, thus improving their status and assisting the total development effort." So I guess we can all go home now! After all, the involvement of women in all projects funded under the Foreign Assistance Act is a law! Public Law 93-189; 87 Statute 714, to be exact.

But having a law on the books is only half the battle. The other half, the big half, is getting the people in charge—in this case, USAID—to pay attention to that law. But make no mistake—our job *is* a little easier thanks to that law.

To push the law further into reality, please write a letter to the president, saying something like this:

George Bush
Executive Office of the President
The White House
1600 Pennsylvania Ave., NW
Washington, DC 20500

Dear Mr. President:
First, congratulations on your show of support to the Peace Corps by pressing for additional funding. It is an extremely positive gesture on your part and I applaud your actions.

But I would like you to do more as well. We are currently between famines in much of the developing world. All the experts insist that this is the time to act—not when there is a crisis underway.

I urge you to enforce those amendments to the Foreign Assistance Act that call for greater involvement of Third World women and protection of the world's forests. I remind you that these charges are law; laws that seem to be ignored right now.

I ask that you instruct USAID to direct its attention entirely toward the kinds of small-scale projects that truly have the potential

to prevent famines before they occur. Water harvesting, the planting of leguminous trees in an alley-cropping system, home gardens
that include a wide variety of native plants, and soil conservation
and restoration techniques will do much to relieve the vulnerability
of the poorest parts of the world to future famines.

It is in the best interest of the United States to get out of the famine relief business and instead expend our energies in the long-
term area of famine prevention.

The result will be U.S. aid funds more intelligently and profit-
ably spent, developing nations that are financially stronger and thus
sooner able to become consumers of U.S. goods and services, a
more peaceful and secure world, and a decrease in worldwide environmental problems related to the spread of the world's deserts.

I urge you to instruct USAID to immediately adopt a more
small-scale, ecologically sound approach—as the Foreign Assistance Act already mandates.

And, once again, congratulations on your strong support of the
Peace Corps. I am only one of many voters who will be anxiously
awaiting your next positive move in support of famine prevention.

Sincerely,

[Signed] _____

Obviously, you have to write your own letter and say what *you*
truly believe. The preceding example is only a guide, and it's probably too long. But that's all right—I have a feeling that you will do
much better when you sit down and compose your letter to the
president.

Remember, so far there really has been no public demand for re-
structuring foreign aid. The head of the foreign relations committee once told me that he couldn't recall anyone writing to tell him
what they thought the United States should or shouldn't do with its
foreign aid funds. Foreign aid is an issue ripe for public involvement—for your involvement. You can do it. Your letters, your

phone calls, your donations, and your involvement can save three lives. Maybe more. Many more.

Here are a few choice quotes you might want to include in your letters or phone conversations:

> We continue to use our aid to build things in the countryside—to build roads, to build dams, to build storage centers—but we haven't yet found a way to get the aid into the environment, into the soil.
>
> And, in fact, looking over a decade of aid to the Sahel, we find that only four percent went to rain-fed agriculture, the way food in the region is grown, and less than 1.5 percent of all those billions of dollars went into the sort of ecological projects which will provide a basis for survivability in the Sahel. (Lloyd Timberlake, in his statement to the House subcommittee hearings on hunger in Africa, 1985 [published in 1987])

> We have learnt to our cost that development which destroys the environment eventually destroys development itself. And we have learnt to our benefit that development that conserves the environment conserves also the fruits of development. (Rajiv Gandhi, prime minister of India, October 19, 1987, in an address to the U.N. General Assembly)

> In 1988 the Worldwatch Institute made rough estimates of the additional expenditures needed to slow population growth, protect topsoil on farmland, reforest the earth, and retire the debt of developing countries—targets it deemed essential to meet for sustained global development by [the year] 2000.
>
> The institute estimated that [these] targets could be achieved with annual expenditures approaching $46 billion in 1990 and increasing to $145 billion in 1994 and $150 billion in 2000.
>
> Meanwhile, the world spends nearly $1 *trillion* a year on military security—more than $2.7 billion a day.
>
> . . . Only an educated and aroused public is likely to force anti-

quated political systems to cooperate in promoting family planning, energy conservation and the protection of the global environment in time to prevent the direst possibilities from occurring. (Alexander Leaf, M.D., chairman of the Department of Preventive Medicine, Harvard Medical School, "Potential Health Effects of Global Climatic and Environmental Changes," *New England Journal of Medicine*, December 7, 1989)

We must take responsibility for preventing and healing what has been so thoughtlessly damaged.

This is not a romantic call for a return to a lost paradise; it is a practical, fundamental matter of survival, not only for hundreds of millions of poor people crushed by poverty but also for all of humanity, to avoid a global ecological disaster.

This problem of conserving the earth while sustaining and improving agricultural production concerns all people because we all share and depend on a single, world-wide ecosystem.

An urgent, committed global effort is required now by both developing and developed countries.

We are all custodians of the earth for future generations. We all share the responsibility for doing the job better than we have done it in the past. (FAO, *Food and the Environment*, A World Food Day issues paper, 1989)

Many present development trends leave increasing numbers of people poor and vulnerable, while at the same time degrading the environment. . . .

We came to see that a new development path was required, one that sustained human progress not just in a few places for a few years, but for the entire planet into the distant future. . . .

We see . . . the possibility for a new era of economic growth, one that must be based on policies that sustain and expand the environmental resources base. And we believe such growth to be absolutely essential to relieve the great poverty that is deepening in much of the developing world. . . . In the final analysis, sustainable development must rest on political will. (Gro Harlem Brundtland, prime minister of Norway, chairperson of the U.N. Commission on Environment and Development, in her committee's report *Our Common Future*, 1987)

The greatest fine art of the future will be the making of a comfortable living from a small piece of land. (Abraham Lincoln)

For some of you, a hundred dollars worth of your time or money may not be enough. You are one of those wonderful people who has the gift of persistence—the desire to keep working at this until you know that you've changed people's minds.

Spend that persistence; invest that life-giving drive in seeing people face to face. When people actually meet you, they are likely to pay even more attention. They are more willing to answer your questions. You can get a real dialogue—an exchange of ideas—going.

You can do this in two ways. First, you can meet with the people we've urged you to write. Arrange meetings with your elected representatives. They will meet with you if you're from the area where they must run for election. If you wish to meet with the people in charge of the various committees we named, ask your representative to arrange this for you. The same goes for charitable organizations. Ask to actually visit with the people in charge. Ask them what you can do to help them achieve these goals. They will be totally disarmed by your approach. Believe me, you can do much in such a situation.

Second, you can use what you know to educate others. You don't need an advanced college degree or a fancy title to be able to speak clearly and compellingly about the aspects of famine prevention. Having read this book, I daresay that you now know more about the real causes of famine and how to prevent it than 99 percent of the so-called development experts out there.

So give a speech on famine prevention. Tell the people who obtain speakers for groups that you're a spokesperson for Rodale Institute's Famine Prevention Project. Because if you've read this book and agree with what we've said, you are. And don't worry about lack of forums. You'll have no trouble being invited to speak. All kinds of local, national, and even international groups are looking for speakers. Start out at your local church, school, community center, YMCA/YWCA, college campus, TV, or radio station. Remember, you've got a dynamite topic.

And if they don't believe that you're a bona fide representative, write to

The Famine Prevention Project
The Rodale Institute
222 Main St.
Emmaus, PA 18098

and we'll send you a letter informing one and all that you *are* a spokesperson for the Famine Prevention Project. No problem.

Remember, people are always willing to listen to someone with practical, low-cost, interesting ideas. And you've got lots of statistics, good science, and some great stories to back you up.

And live your own stories. Do what I did. Remember, no one sent me to Mexico back in 1949. I went because I wanted to see what it was like. And that trip was one of the most profound, enjoyable, illuminating experiences of my young life.

So go to Mexico. But not to Cancun—rent a jeep and drive through the villages. Take the rural route that I took way back when. See a part of the Third World for yourself. I bet you'll come away with as strong a feeling for the people as I did.

Or go to Africa. But not to some game preserve to take pictures of giraffes. Visit small farms in villages you never heard of. Make a few friends and travel around. Go to a place where people live and wait for each new morning. See the currents of life quicken with the dawn.

Don't flash a camera. You'll remember more clearly if you use your eyes. I have a million perfect images of Africa in my head. They made me write this book. What will the images you bring home make *you* do?

I'll tell you one thing—a visit to the Third World will make you ten times more credible to any audience. You'll have real clout. Imagine telling a person who schedules speakers for a community college that you just got back from Africa and want to discuss famine prevention. You just shot to the top of the list.

Or try your elected representative. Or the head of a charitable organization. "Why do you want to see me?" they might ask.

"Well, I just got back from a village in Africa where I saw that the way your funds are being used is actually contributing to the infant death rate, and I wanted to discuss this with you first before I started speaking about it publicly. . . ." (How fast do you think you're going to get an appointment?)

Don't have the money to travel? Join the Peace Corps. It's already 90 percent in tune with what we're doing, and I've never heard former volunteers say anything other than that it was the most amazing, enjoyable, and energizing experience of their lives.

Only have a little money to travel? Come to Pennsylvania and visit the Rodale Institute's Research Center, where we constantly test these solutions in our own experimental fields (at a total cost of somewhere over $12 million so far—just in case you were wondering if I'd tossed in my own $100 yet). Write to the Famine Prevention Project and schedule your visit. We'll give you a tour and help you put together a speaking program or discuss your other options for further action.

Or you might raise the money to join us or a similar group on a fact-finding trip to a Third World country. I've led such groups

myself, and I know that other organizations have hosted similar ventures. Contact your church, school, or community organizations—even your family and friends—and get sponsored.

Begin to do these things and you will discover your own capacity to be a leader. You have the potential to turn on as many people to the concept of famine prevention as I do. I wouldn't mind if you did even better. And remember, if you need help, guidance, credentials, or want to add to our store of information and ideas, just contact the Famine Prevention Project.

No matter how well I've done, you are the strongest link in the chain that is needed to end famine forever. I now turn the podium over to you. Step right up.

Finally, here is a partial listing of organizations actively involved in the fight against hunger. You may want to write to one or several of them to express your views about the need for long-term sustainable projects to prevent famine, and to determine just how committed they are to that approach.

Please remember that inclusion of a group on this list does not necessarily constitute our endorsement of it. You should make your own decision about which organizations you might wish to support with time or money, based on their responses to your letters.

AFRICARE
440 R Street, NW
Washington, DC 20001
(202) 462-3614

American Friends
    Service Committee
1501 Cherry Street
Philadelphia, PA 19102
(215) 241-7000

Bread for the World
802 Rhode Island Avenue,
    NE
Washington, DC 20018
(202) 269-0200

CARE
660 First Avenue
New York, NY 10016
(212) 686-3110

Catholic Relief Services
209 West Fayette Street
Baltimore, MD 21201
(301) 625-2220

Church World Service
457 Riverside Drive
New York, NY 10115
(212) 870-2257

Food for the Hungry
7729 E. Greenway Road
Scottsdale, AZ 85260
(602) 998-3100

Global Tomorrow Coalition
1325 G Street, NW, Suite 915
Washington, DC 20005
(202) 628-4016

Heifer Project International
P.O. Box 808
Little Rock, AR 72203
(501) 376-6836

The Hunger Project
1 Madison Avenue
New York, NY 10010
(212) 532-4255

International Voluntary Services
1424 16th Street, NW, Suite 204
Washington, DC 20036
(202) 387-5533

Overseas Education Fund
1815 H Street, NW, 11th
   Floor
Washington, DC 20006
(202) 466-3430

Oxfam America
115 Broadway
Boston, MA 02116
(617) 482-1211

Population Institute
110 Maryland Avenue, NE
Washington, DC 20002
(202) 544-3300

The Rodale Institute
Famine Prevention Project
222 Main Street
Emmaus, PA 18098-0015
(215) 967-5171

Save the Children Federation
54 Wilton Road
Westport, CT 06880
(203) 226-7271

UNICEF
3 U.N. Plaza
New York, NY 10017
(212) 326-7000

U.S. Peace Corps
1990 K Street NW
Washington, DC 20526
(202) 606-3886

Volunteers in Technical
   Assistance (VITA)
1815 N. Lynn Street
Arlington, VA 22209
(703) 276-1800

World Policy Institute
777 U.N. Plaza
New York, NY 10017
(212) 490-0010

World Resources Institute
1709 New York Avenue, NW,
   Suite 700
Washington, DC 20006
(202) 638-6300

Worldwatch Institute
1776 Massachusetts Avenue,
   NW, Suite 701
Washington, DC 20036
(202) 452-1999

Bibliography

Anderson, Edgar. *Plants, Man and Life*. Berkeley: University of California Press, 1952.

Brown, Lester R., and others. *State of the World 1989*. New York: Norton, 1989.

Chen, Y. S., and others. "Alley Cropping Vegetable Crops with *Leucaena* in Southern Nigeria." *HortScience,* October 1989, pp. 839–840.

The Conservation Foundation. *State of the Environment: A View Toward the Nineties*. Washington, DC: The Conservation Foundation, 1987.

Cramer, Craig, and others (eds.). *The Farmer's Fertilizer Handbook*. Emmaus, PA: Regenerative Agriculture Association, 1986.

Curtis, Donald, Michael Hubbard, and Andrew Shepherd. *Preventing Famine: Policies and Prospects for Africa*. New York: Routledge, Chapman and Hall, 1988.

Dover, Michael J., and Lee M. Talbot. *To Feed the Earth: Agro-Ecology for Sustainable Development*. Washington, DC: World Resources Institute, 1987.

Ellis, William S. "A Soviet Sea Lies Dying." *National Geographic,* February 1990, pp. 73–92.

Estava, Gustavo. "Cease Aid and Stop Development: An Answer to Hunger." Paper presented at the International Seminar on Food and Efficiency, CEESTEM-UNESCO, Aug. 6–9, 1985.

Faculty of Agriculture, Forestry and Veterinary Science of the University of Dar es Salaam, Morogoro, Tanzania. *Resource-Efficient Farming Methods for Tanzania.* Emmaus, PA: Rodale Press, 1983.

Food and Agriculture Organization. *Protect and Produce: Soil Conservation for Development.* Rome: FAO, 1983.

Food and Agriculture Organization. *Food and the Environment.* Rome: FAO, 1989.

Gall, Norman. "Shunning Map to Prosperity, Vast Nations Take the Low Road." *Wall Street Journal,* May 31, 1989.

Gedda, George. "U.S. Faults Ethiopia Rebel Action." *Philadelphia Inquirer,* February 20, 1990.

Ghebremeskel, K. "The State of Food Production and Nutrition in the Developing Countries." *Nutrition and Health,* 6 (3), 1989, 121–128.

Gibson, I. A. S. and T. Jones. "Monoculture as the Origin of Major Forest Pests and Diseases." In J. M. Cherett and G. R. Sager (eds.), *Origins of Pest, Parasite, and Weed Problems.* The 18th symposium of the British Ecological Society. Oxford, England: Blackwell Scientific, 1976.

Gilbert, Henry. *The Neem Tree: An Inhibitor of Insect Feeding and Growth, 1982–1989.* Beltsville, MD: U.S. Department of Agriculture, 1989.

Greene, Graham. *Journey Without Maps.* New York: Penguin USA, 1978.

Howard, Sir Albert. *An Agricultural Testament.* New York: Oxford University Press, 1943.

International Crops Research Institute for the Semi-Arid Tropics. *Soil, Crop and Water Management in the Sudano-Sahelian Zone.* Andrha Pradesh, India: ICRISAT, 1989.

International Institute of Tropical Agriculture. *Alley Cropping: A Stable Alternative to Shifting Cultivation.* London: Balding & Mansell, 1986.

King, F. H. *Farmers of Forty Centuries.* Emmaus, PA: Rodale Press, 1911.

Leaf, Alexander, M.D. "Potential Health Effects of Global Climatic and Environmental Changes." *New England Journal of Medicine,* December 7, 1989, pp. 1577–1583.

Martin, F. W., and L. Telek. *Vegetables for the hot, humid tropics.* Part 6.

Amaranthus and Celosia. New Orleans: U.S. Department of Agriculture, 1979.

McGrath, Mike. "Bugs for Sale." *Organic Gardening,* August 1984, pp. 34–43.

National Academy of Sciences, National Research Council. *Amaranth: Modern Prospects for an Ancient Crop.* Emmaus, PA: Rodale Press, 1985.

National Academy of Sciences, National Research Council. "Underexploited Indigenous Crops of Africa." Washington, DC: NAS-NRC, 1989.

National Academy of Sciences, National Research Council. "Vetiver Grass: Possible New Measure for Reducing Soil Erosion." Washington, DC: NAS-NRC, 1989.

Nour, Jane, and others. "Africa in the Grip of Witchweed." *New Scientist,* January 9, 1986, pp. 44–48.

Okigbo, Bede N. "Broadening the Food Base in Africa: The Potential of Traditional Food Plants." *Food and Nutrition, 12* (1), 1986, 4–17.

Paarlberg, Don. *Toward a Well-Fed World.* Ames: Iowa State University Press, 1988.

Pootier, J. P. "The Politics of Famine Prevention: Ecology, Regional Production and Food Complementarity in Western Rwanda." *African Affairs: Journal of the Royal African Society, 85* (339), 1986, 207–237.

Reid, Walter V., and others. *Bankrolling Successes: A Portfolio of Sustainable Development Projects.* Washington, DC: Environmental Policy Institute, and National Wildlife Federation, 1988.

Reid, Walter V., and Kenton R. Miller. *Keeping Options Alive: The Scientific Basis for Conserving Biodiversity.* Washington, DC: World Resources Institute, 1989.

Rodale Institute. *Enough Food: Achieving Food Security Through Regenerative Agriculture.* Emmaus, PA: Rodale Institute, 1985.

Sattaur, Omar. "The Shrinking Gene Pool." *New Scientist,* July 29, 1989, pp. 37–41.

Schneider, Keith. "Science Academy Says Chemicals Do Not Necessarily Increase Crops." *New York Times,* September 8, 1989.

The Hunger Project. *Famine and Chronic Persistent Hunger: A Life and Death Distinction.* New York: The Hunger Project, 1989. (video)

Timberlake, Lloyd. *Africa in Crisis: The Causes, the Cures of Environmen-*

tal Bankruptcy. Washington, DC: International Institute for Environment and Development, 1985.

Timberlake, Lloyd. "The Politics of Food Aid." In M. Beazley (ed.), *The Earth Report.* Los Angeles: Price Stern Sloan, 1988.

U.S. Department of Agriculture. *Techniques and Plants for the Tropical Subsistence Farm.* Beltsville, MD: USDA, 1980.

Subcommittee on Natural Resources, Agriculture Research, and Environment, U.S. House Committee on Science, Space, and Technology. *Prospects for Sustainable Development in Sub-Saharan Africa.* Washington, DC: U.S. Government Printing Office, 1987.

Winser, Nigel. *The Sea of Sands and Mists.* London: Century Hutchinson, 1989.

World Hunger Education Service. *Who's Involved with Hunger: An Organization Guide for Education and Advocacy.* 4th ed. Washington, DC: World Hunger Education Service, 1985.

World Resources Institute and International Institute for Environment and Development. *World Resources 1988–89: An Assessment of the Resource Base That Supports the Global Economy.* New York: Basic Books, 1988.

Index